Silly Scribbles

A Complete Readiness Program for Young Children

Shirley A. Steinmetz

Illustrations by Eileen Gerne Ciavarella
Based on original drawings by
Shirley A. Steinmetz

THE CENTER FOR APPLIED
RESEARCH IN EDUCATION
West Nyack, New York 10995

10 9 8 7 6 5 4 3 2 1

Printed in the United States of America

Library of Congress Cataloging-in-Publication Data

Steinmetz, Shirley A.
    Silly scribbles : complete readiness program for young children /
illustrations by Eileen Gerne Ciavarella; based on original
drawings by Shirley A. Steinmetz.
        p. cm.
    ISBN 0-87628-776-3
    1. Reading readiness.   2. Reading (Kindergarten)   3. Reading
(Preschool)   I. Title.
LB1181.35.S74   1988
372.4—dc19   88-25732
                                                                  CIP

ISBN 0-87628-776-3

THE CENTER FOR APPLIED
RESEARCH IN EDUCATION
BUSINESS & PROFESSIONAL DIVISION
A division of Simon & Schuster
West Nyack, New York 10995

DEDICATION

This book is dedicated to all the children who loved Stan and Carla and doing Silly Scribbles so much, that this collection became the beginning.

ACKNOWLEDGMENTS

A special thank you to:

Susan Klotz, my friend with so much knowledge and support.

Jean Jacobsen, my friend who could spell and proofread every page.

Eric Jacobsen, my friend who gave helpful suggestions.

Virginia McGavin and Virginia Rita who always knew it would happen and started and stayed with me along the way.

Chuck, my husband, who did it all while I was in the office working.

Shannon, my daughter, who learned to fix her own dinner and gave many helpful suggestions.

All the teachers and principals who gave their support.

ABOUT THE AUTHOR

Shirley A. Steinmetz received her B.S. in Elementary Education from Western Michigan University. She has been involved in teaching for over seventeen years.
Mrs. Steinmetz is currently teaching kindergarten for the Fairfax County Public Schools in Reston, Virginia.

ABOUT THIS BOOK

The concept for *Silly Scribbles: A Complete Readiness Program for Young Children* started simply as an enjoyable way to practice the basic strokes needed for letter formation that otherwise seemed so monotonous.

Completing a Silly Scribble involves the total child in an activity that is so enjoyable and gives the child such a sense of pride and accomplishment, that the essential readiness skills being developed become incidental to the enjoyment. These skills include:

- organization and preparation
- ability to determine direction (top/bottom, left/right, up/down, inside/outside, over/under)
- recognition of colors, basic shapes, similarities/differences, and patterns
- an understanding of number concepts, time, weather, and seasons
- ability to use given clues and past experiences or knowledge to predict outcomes
- increase of attention span, eye-hand development, and fine-motor coordination

Silly Scribbles is divided into four sections. The first section offers complete directions to the teacher in presenting the material to students. In this section, you will also find a progress report and a letter you can send to parents that describes the program.

Section 2 gives 102 Silly Scribbles you can do in the skill areas of color recognition, shape recognition, and letter recognition and sound-letter correspondence. Each two-page Silly Scribble has a teacher-directed page with suggested activities, followed by the Silly Scribble.

Since *Silly Scribbles* is geared to be a success-oriented program for each child, you will find three different skill levels of Silly Scribbles:

- Level I is the simplest Silly Scribble and all children may do these. Level I will usually be made with simple basic shapes for easier line formation. If a child is frustrated with Level I, you may find it necessary to make a START line for each child on his or her paper to give a base to build from. You may also fold your paper and the child's to give concrete divisions of space.
- Level II is of moderate difficulty, but can be done slowly with one line at a time.
- Level III is the most difficult, but you may find children who can do these easily with slow and positive guidance.

Section 3 is the story *Friends* that can be reproduced and given to each child to take home and share.

Section 4 consists of a full-page worksheet for each letter of the alphabet. Children are given the opportunity to practice writing the upper- and lower-case letters.

Remember that *Silly Scribbles* has been designed to reinforce basic developmental skills for use in reading and written language. Silly Scribbles is not art! Doing Silly Scribbles should never replace self-expression or the child's experience of creating on his or her own with paint, crayons, glue, scissors, or other mediums. This program is not meant to dictate to any child what something should look like or what color something must be. It is the process of making straight and curved lines, not the end product that is most important to developing readiness skills. Keep in mind, however, that because children are instructed to copy teacher-drawn pictures and strokes exactly, some may respond by accepting these teacher-made images as correct, best, or the only way to draw a house, fish, or teddy bear. Therefore, you must emphasize that each of these drawings is just one way to make that object. It is important that you then encourage the children to make their own, unique interpretations with follow-up activities using paint, markers, paper and glue, clay, or other mediums.

Please note that the Silly Scribbles are not meant to be reproduced as individual worksheets and handed to the children to do on their own. It is the "process" of following the teacher by drawing lines on their own paper that makes this program so unique and enjoyable to children.

It is my hope that you may find *Silly Scribbles* enjoyable and easy to follow, that you can integrate Silly Scribbles into your program easily — and most of all that you may help a child feel that indeed learning is fun!

Shirley A. Steinmetz

CONTENTS

Letter Recognition and Sound-Letter Correspondence ● 62

Section 1
DIRECTIONS FOR THE TEACHER

Since it is the teacher who first makes the lines that the children will copy, using the same color, size, and placement, it is important that you be given specific directions so that you feel comfortable doing "Silly Scribbles" — even if you feel you cannot draw. Basically, all you need to remember is that you are really only making straight or curved lines, just one line at a time. They don't have to be perfect — just fun. So, don't panic, because the following pages are meant for *you*!

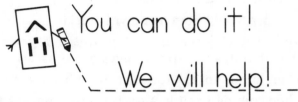

HOW TO DO SILLY SCRIBBLES

Silly Scribbles is the simple process of playing "follow the teacher" with crayons and paper. The child simply makes lines on his or her own paper by watching and then making every line you make on your paper. The child uses the same color and number, and tries to make it as close to the same size and placement as yours. Perfection is not expected by either you or the child.

At the Beginning of the School Year

Make a copy of the story "Friends" (see Section 3) for each child. Read the story and color with the children: . . . . . dotted Carla lines are green, and ----- dash Stan lines are blue. Let the children take the books home to share and keep.

Introduce your students to Stan and Carla classroom activities:

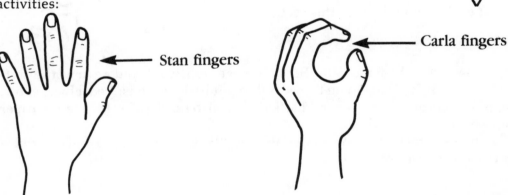

1. Look around the classroom and find Stan lines (for example, the chalkboard).

2. Look around the classroom and find Carla lines (for example, the clock).

3. Play "Stan fingers, Carla fingers":

    a. Ask the children to show you how their fingers would make a Stan line. A Carla line.

    b. How about Stan arms? Carla arms? (a hug)

    c. How about a Stan back? A Carla back?

    d. How about Stan legs? Carla legs?

    e. Feet? One finger? Whole body? Mouth?

    f. How would Stan stand up? Carla?

    g. How would Stan sit down? Carla?

    h. How would Stan jump? Carla?

    i. How would Stan lie down? Carla?

    When the children are antsy, this is a great way to move around for a few minutes and strengthen small muscles and develop body awareness.

4. When lining up, ask for a "straight Stan line."

5. When coming to sit in a circle on the rug, ask for a nice "Carla circle."

6. Reinforce Stan straight and Carla curve whenever you can throughout your time with the children.

After reading "Friends" and doing classroom activities, you and your students are ready to begin Silly Scribbles.

Silly Scribble Groups

Establish your Silly Scribble groups by grouping the children according to:

1. How well the child can write his or her own name.

2. How each child draws a picture of him- or herself (most mature to immature).

3. How each child fits into a particular skill level as described in "Silly Scribble Skill Levels" found later in this section.

What You Need

Choose the right-hand Silly Scribble page you want and review the left-hand teacher-directed page. You'll need only eight basic crayons: red, blue, yellow, green, purple, brown, orange, and black. You'll also need 12" x 18" manila paper (*not* newsprint) for each child.

For more information on materials, see "How to Set Up a Silly Scribble Center" later in this section.

What to Think About

An important readiness skill that should be developed by a young child is practice of the basic strokes used in forming letters for use in written language. Therefore, it is very important when making any line that you want the children to follow that you *"model" the correct line direction.*

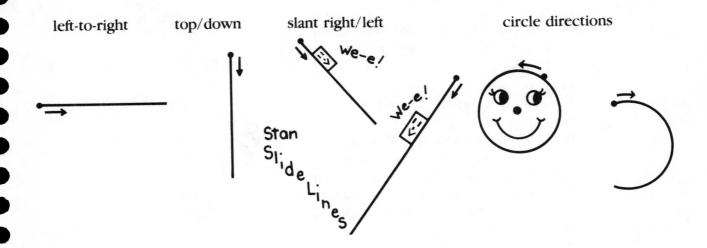

| left-to-right | top/down | slant right/left | circle directions |

Left-to-Right Movement

To encourage the children in using left-to-right movement while writing their names, give them a visual clue by making a COLORED STAR in the left-hand corner of *your* paper.

1. When the children look at the colored star on your paper, they will be able to tell *where* to write their name on their own paper and *what color* to use while writing their name. (If you have children who cannot write their own name, either write it for them or use dotted lines and have them trace over it. Always encourage them to try!)

2. By looking at your paper, the children will also be able to determine the direction in which to place their own paper: "standing up" or "lying down." Have the children pretend they are the piece of paper you are holding in your hands. See if they can determine whether they should be standing up or lying down, according to which direction you turn the piece of manila paper. Practice this a few times, and the children will know quickly which way their paper should be placed.

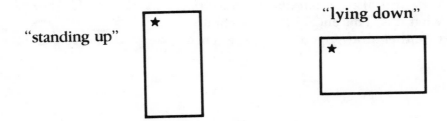

"standing up"   "lying down"

Colors

Do your students know colors?

1. Hold up a crayon and tell the children this is the color they will need. Review holding up each color until they know; if you hold up a red, they would also need to get a red. (Children love to keep up with you and not get "tricked," so go through each color several times, each time going faster to see if anyone gets "tricked.")

2. Explain that from now on, they will need to *watch* for when you change crayons. You will not be reminding them each time.

3. Remind the children that they will be doing Silly Scribbles using Stan and Carla lines to make something fun. Each time they must make on their own paper the same line you made on yours using the same colored crayon.

4. Always pause each time before getting a new crayon to give the children time to catch up.

gotcha!

Review One More Time

Remind the children of Stan straight lines and Carla curved lines from the story "Friends."

Explain that you are going to be making something fun together called Silly Scribbles using Stan and Carla lines. The children must do *what you do* using the same color!

1. Make the START line on your paper and say, "I have made a line like this. Can you do the same on your paper?" (You may want to make the START line on a child's paper if he or she is having difficulty in placement.)

2. *Do not tell the children what it will be.* (You may give clues, such as it begins with "b" or is brown.)

3. Encourage the children to guess when they think they know what it is. The children love to be the one who guesses first. You might want to say "BINGO!" when they do. As they watch and do, they will also be *thinking and wondering* what it is. This encourages the children to either draw upon past experiences

Bingo!

It's Carla!

or use clues to predict outcome. Even if the child does not know what the Silly Scribble is, he or she will often seek to find out more about it.

Go Slow! Make Each Line One at a Time

In the beginning, talk the children through each line: "I am making a red line down."

1. Remind the children when you have a new color. "Now what color do I have?"

2. Correct quietly and positively. "Is my circle bigger or smaller?" "Which color did I use?" "What way does my line go?" "It is okay this time, but next time watch more closely."

As time goes on, talk will lessen and the children will just watch and do. They soon will be "silent" Silly Scribblers.

A SILLY SCRIBBLE SAMPLE ACTIVITY

Begin each school year by reviewing one color a week. This way you can check to see if each child knows the colors or even suffers from color blindness.

Below is a sample activity. Begin the line at the dot • . Make each line slowly and pause each time to emphasize the starting point.

<u>Color recognition:</u> red	<u>Paper direction:</u> lying down
<u>Star color:</u> red	<u>Silly Scribble:</u> wagon

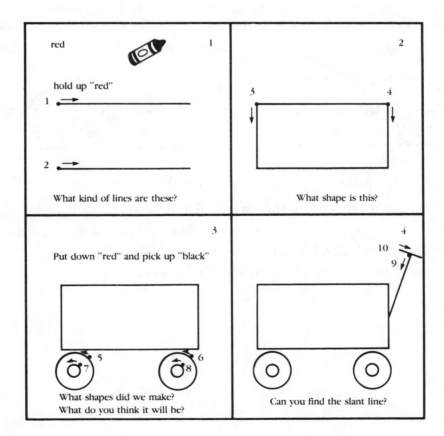

Children will do better if they make lines on both sides. Going back and forth from side to side seems to give them a sense of balance and proportion. So if you cannot find the next number, just look across to the other side.

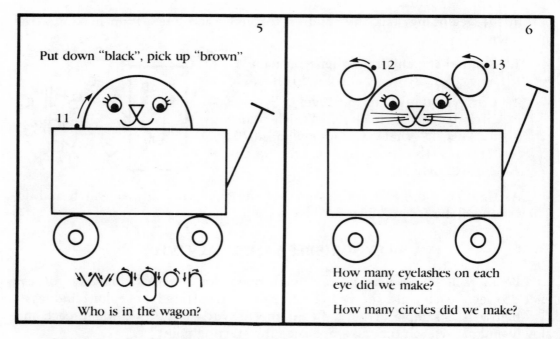

Always write what the Silly Scribble is as the final step. Form each letter with one line at a time. Use basic letter formation strokes. You may want to encourage some children to try and write what it is themselves. It is *not* expected that the children will be able to read these words. It is simply another way of exposing the children to the printed word while developing vocabulary.

You can change what is in the wagon by changing the shape of the ears!

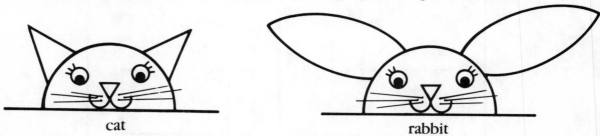

Here are some questions you can ask during this Silly Scribble:

1. Where is the animal? (in the wagon, above the rectangle)
2. How many whiskers? (will vary depending on how many you draw)
3. Where are the wheels? (under the rectangle, at the bottom)
4. Where is the rectangle? (in the middle, between)

HOW TO SET UP A SILLY SCRIBBLE CENTER

When setting up a Silly Scribble center, you will need only a few things:

1. table for group to sit at with own space or own desk
2. easel, chalkboard, or wall to put the teacher's paper on so all children can see clearly each line made
3. your own set of eight basic crayons
4. manila paper to distribute to each child

When the children get to your center:

1. Tell them they will be doing Silly Scribbles.
2. Explain that they will need these colors: red, blue, purple, green, orange, yellow, brown, black.
3. Explain that each time they come to do Silly Scribbles, they must do the following:

   a. Get out the eight basic colors and lay them on the table.
   b. Look at the teacher's page.
   c. Determine "standing up" or "lying down."
   d. Determine the color and placement of the "star" in the left corner of the teacher's paper and write their name on their own paper in that color.
   e. Wait quietly until everyone else is ready.
4. You are ready to begin.

Encourage the children to remember all the steps by putting a happy face or stamp by the child's name who has done all the steps without being reminded. It won't take long before everyone is ready on time.

Have a broken crayon box nearby for the child who is missing a color. It is the child's responsibility to make sure he or she has the eight colors needed to do a Silly Scribble.

When doing the Silly Scribble, use the entire 12" x 18" sheet of paper. Make it BIG, which is easier for the young learner.

SILLY SCRIBBLE SKILL LEVELS

As you know, children are developmentally mature at different times. Consequently, three skill levels are used in Silly Scribbles. Since Silly Scribbles is geared to individual needs, be aware of the frustration level and place the children accordingly.

Determine Skill Level Groups

1. How well can the child write his or her name?   Stan
    a. uses upper case and lower case   STAN
    b. uses upper case only
    c. knows a few letters in own name or none at all
2. Have each child draw a self-portrait.
    a. determine groups by number of details included
    b. date and keep each for comparison of growth

Determine Size of Silly Scribble Group

The younger the child, the smaller the group.

Determine Appropriate Skill Level

1. Level I: preschool and kindergarten
    a. smallest group size
    b. simplest Silly Scribbles
    c. all children may begin with or use Level I
2. Level II: kindergarten and first grade
    a. moderate-size group
    b. moderate difficulty
3. Level III: kindergarten and first grade
    a. large group or whole class
    b. most complicated detail

What You Can Do If a Child
Is Having Difficulty With Placement

1. Make the START line on the child's paper to give him or her a place to begin and build from. The child does the rest.
2. Fold the paper into thirds so the child has guide lines to help with placement.
3. *Always go slowly* and point out things to look for or give directions while making the line so the child has a chance to see what is happening.

SILLY SCRIBBLES AS A DIAGNOSTIC TOOL

Observing each child while making Silly Scribbles can be a wonderful diagnostic tool. This can help you with early identification of the following skills:

1. Does the child know:
    a. colors?   red   blue   green

b. shapes?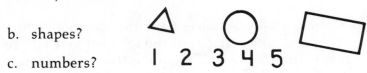

c. numbers?

2. How does the child hold the crayon?
3. What hand does the child consistently use?
4. Can the child find patterns?
5. Can the child remember sequence?
6. How is the quality of reproduction?
    a. Does the child make lines from the top-down?
    b. Does the child makes lines from left to right?
7. Can the child draw from past experience to predict outcome?
8. Can the child predict given clues of beginning sounds?
9. Is the child frustrated?
    a. Reevaluate the skill level
10. Does the child experience any visual or perceptual problems?
    a. Does the child need glasses?

Check with the school nurse or special teachers for help on evaluating major problems you see.

WAYS TO ENCOURAGE CREATIVITY

It is the aim of this program to use Stan straight lines and Carla curved lines to practice the correct strokes needed in letter formation while developing readiness skills. This program is not meant to be used in place of art where children are encouraged to use their own imaginations to create expressive, personal drawings, paintings, sculpture, collages, and other projects. In order that the children do not respond to the following of lines to make silly pictures as the only correct way to make that object, it is recommended that you emphasize to the children that this is only *one way* of making that object. After finishing the Silly Scribble, encourage the children to discuss, share, and seek other ways for creating the same object using their own individual creative expression. Here are suggested ways to help you do this:

1. Discuss other ways to make various parts of the Silly Scribble you have just done. How could you make the nose different? How would you make it look mean instead of happy?
2. Have the children turn the Silly Scribble paper over and draw what they think the other side of this object looks like. For example, for the monkey that is drawn with its back to you, what does the front look like?
3. Look at many different versions of the same stories (*Three Billy Goats Gruff*, for example) and compare how different illustrators have drawn the same things in different ways. Each is individual and different.

4. After you have done a Silly Scribble, have the children compare their own Silly Scribbles and notice that even though everyone was following teacher-drawn lines, there are still unique differences. (In fact, theirs are usually cuter than yours!)

5. Have a child describe to another person the different steps that were taken to make the Silly Scribble.

6. Set up an art center with paper, scissors, markers, crayons, fingerpaints, scrap paper, fabric scraps, glue, easel and paint, and clay and let the children make their own pictures of the Silly Scribbles they have done.

7. Let the children cut out pictures from magazines that depict all aspects that are relevant to the Silly Scribble they have done. Encourage them to make a collage.

8. Use a junk collection (buttons for eyes or toothpicks for quills) to make their Silly Scribble "come alive."

9. Create a home for an animal that was used in the Silly Scribble. You can use a shoe box.

10. Whenever you have the chance, bring in a real object like the silly Scribble done the day before. It is important to do this *after* the scribble activity because you don't want to take away the opportunity for the children to predict and anticipate. Many of the Silly Scribbles can easily be brought in, such as a wagon, rabbit, ball, watermelon, and the like. Have the children touch, explore, and discuss where there are straight or curved lines, then try and draw, paint, sculpt or cut and paste their own version.

11. Look anywhere for information to share with the children about the Silly Scribble. You can check encyclopedias, dictionaries, nature magazines and books, *National Geographic*, videos, movies, filmstrips, stories, and even special guests.

12. Always encourage the children to SEE not only with their eyes but with all their senses.

13. Let the children make their own suggestions on what they could or would like to do.

14. Remember that all of these apply to you, the teacher, as well. Be creative!

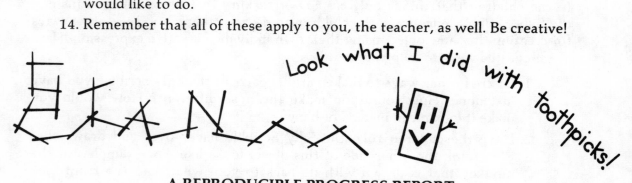

A REPRODUCIBLE PROGRESS REPORT

The following progress chart is for the teacher who wishes to keep a record of the progress the students have made in the developmental skill areas covered by doing Silly Scribbles. The progress report is to be used only as a diagnostic tool to determine which skills the child can accomplish and which need more reinforcement. Silly Scribbles should not be used as an art lesson and should never replace a chance for the child to express his or her own creativity. It is important that you emphasize to the child that doing a Silly Scribble is only one way of making that object. This program was designed to help the child practice readiness skills, while practicing the straight and curved lines used in letter formation. It is important that everything the child does be received with a positive outlook. Every child should feel successful at Silly Scribbles; some will just need more reinforcement of a given skill.

A LETTER TO PARENTS

Because parents of the young learner have a special interest in what is happening in their child's classroom, a reproducible letter is included here for you to send home. This letter gives the parents information about Stan and Carla and doing Silly Scribbles. You may want to send the letter home with the story "Friends" or use it as a handout during your back-to-school night.

SILLY SCRIBBLE PROGRESS REPORT

Name _____   left-handed   right-handed

Comments: 1   observed growth from September to November
              2   observed growth from November to January

Skills being observed:

	1	2
uses the correct color		
makes the same number of lines		
can find geometric shapes in the Silly Scribble (rectangle, square, circle, and triangle)		
makes placement of lines on the paper same as the teacher		
top	___	___
middle	___	___
bottom	___	___
left side	___	___
right side	___	___
child can locate line placement made when asked		
over	___	___
under	___	___
inside	___	___
outside	___	___
beside	___	___

Follows the same line direction as the teacher:

+ If child makes line moving in same direction as teacher.
✓ Only if child consistently moves in opposite direction as teacher.

	1		2	
circle	⤾ ccw	⤿ cw	⤾ ccw	⤿ cw
horizontal	→ right	← left	→ right	← left
vertical	↑ up	↓ down	↑ up	↓ down
slant	↘ right	↗ left	↘ right	↗ left

(continued)

Name _____

SILLY SCRIBBLE PROGRESS REPORT (continued)

Skills being observed:	1	2
has attention span to follow without getting behind		
does not get distracted . . . stays on task		
knows the difference between a straight and curved line		
can make a straight or curved line without difficulty		
given clues, can predict what Silly Scribble will be		
seems to have developed better eye-hand skills		
seems to have developed better fine-motor skills		
can follow or make left-to-right movement		
seems to have a better concept of space		
can remember sequence of line placement		
has developed a better sense of size (which is bigger? smaller? same size?)		
enjoys doing Silly Scribbles		

*Note to teachers . . . Silly Scribbles is not to be used as an art lesson and should never replace a chance for the child to express his or her own creativity. It is important that you emphasize to the child that doing a Silly Scribble is only one way of making that object. This program was designed to help the child practice all the skills listed above, while practicing the straight and curved lines used in letter formation. It is important that everything the child does be received with a positive outlook! This progress report is to be used as a diagnostic tool to determine which skills the child can accomplish and which need more reinforcement. Every child should feel successful at Silly Scribbles; some will just need more reinforcement of a given skill.

+   Observed child working at developmental level

✓   Observed child needing more practice of this skill

NA   Have not observed child on this skill

Dear Parents,

This year, your child will be participating in a "success-oriented" program designed to promote the learning of many developmental readiness skills used in written language. This program is called SILLY SCRIBBLES.

To find out how Silly Scribbles came to be, you must read your take-home copy of Stan and Carla in "Friends" with your child. You will find that Stan is a straight line and Carla is a curved line. Because each has talents that make it unique and special (like all people), Stan and Carla decide to play together and share their special skills to the delight of the children. After getting to know Stan and Carla well as our friends, we will start the program called Silly Scribbles, where we can use Stan straight line and Carla curved line to make silly pictures. Your child simply plays "follow the leader" with crayons using the same color, making the same size and placement on the paper as the teacher.

So many developmental skills are strengthened by doing Silly Scribbles and knowing Stan and Carla, that we will be referring to our new friends throughout the school year. The following are some of the readiness developmental skills that are reinforced by this program: color, shape, and letter recognition; number concepts; sound-letter correspondence; visual placement; similarities and differences; ability to predict outcomes given clues; vocabulary development; body awareness; "I am special too"; and many other basic concepts. In fact, by doing Silly Scribbles, your child is simply practicing the proper basic strokes used in correct letter formation — but in a fun way.

The one thing I want to stress to you is that this *is not art*! This program will not be used in place of art where children are encouraged to use their own imagination to create beautiful, expressive, personal drawing, painting, sculpture, collages, and projects. In order that a child not respond to the following of lines to make silly pictures as the only correct way to make that object, it will be emphasized by the teacher that this is only one of many ways to make the drawing, and encouragement will be given to discuss, share, and seek other ways. It is the goal of this program to practice straight and curved lines used in letter formation and development of readiness skills, while always allowing individual creative expression. So please keep in mind, when you see the Silly Scribbles coming home, that it is not how good the finished product looks, but the process of making it that is important!

You can help your child by asking questions about the picture and how it was made, such as:

"Tell me which line you made first?" (second? last?)
"What shape is that? How many did you make in this picture?"
"What color did you use for the square?" (rectangle? circle? oval?)

"How many eyelashes did you make on each eye?" (all together?)
"What is at the top?" (middle? left side? right side?)
"What is above this line?" (below? inside? beside?)
"Which line is Carla?" "Which is Stan?"
"Which is bigger?" (smaller? the same size?)

Each week we will be doing Silly Scribbles that have either the beginning sound of the week or the shape, color, or theme of that week. We must admit that at times we can't help but smile at the fun the children will have with Silly Scribbles. Can you imagine their reaction if we told them they were learning something while having fun?

Stan   Carla

MORE SILLY SCRIBBLES ACTIVITIES

1. Look everywhere! Your clothes, toys, room, shoes, crayons, paper, face, in books, rocks, trees, clouds, and so forth, and find Stan lines and Carla lines. Touch and feel them if you can.

2. When the children use clay, can they make a Stan line? A Carla line?

3. While playing with clay, have the children use various implements (spools, toothpicks, cut-off sections of straws, spoons, forks, pieces of heavy thread) to press designs or patterns of straight and/or curved lines into a flattened piece of clay.

4. Take a walk around your classroom, school, or playground. Have the children find as many things as they can made by a Stan line or a Carla line. Be sure to let the children touch if possible. When you get back to the classroom, have the children discuss what they saw and draw a picture if they can. Display these on a bulletin board or make a small book.

5. Whenever the children are having a snack, discuss who makes the lines in that snack — Stan or Carla? If you bite into a square cracker, who makes the bite mark.

6. Play "Where Is Stan (or Carla)?" Make a small posterboard Stan (or Carla) and while the children cover their eyes, hide Stan somewhere in the room. Let some part of him stick out so the children can see where he is by looking. The child who can give the correct description of where Stan is hiding gets to hide him the next time. Look for words that tell direction or placement, such as "Stan is *under* the red apple" or "Stan is *behind* the eraser on the teacher's desk." This game encourages the children to use whole sentences and basic comprehension skills.

7. When playing with blocks, puzzles, shapes, beads, letters, numbers, and the like, sort them into three piles: those made by Stan alone, those by Carla alone, and those by Carla and Stan together. Let the children "feel" the difference. Can they do it with their eyes closed? This activity helps with sorting and classifying skills.

8. You can easily make a Stan and Carla letter game by taking a piece of posterboard and making a game trail. Put a letter in each space. On an extra wooden cube, make Stan by himself, Carla by herself, and Stan and Carla together. (Two of each will cover all sides.) The child then rolls the wooden cube to see what kind of letter he or she moves to. This game will reinforce letter formation. (You can also make bingo cards using the letters and the same die. The child who covers a row first wins.)

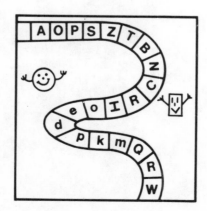

Section 2
SILLY SCRIBBLES ACTIVITIES

In this section you will find Silly Scribbles activities for color recognition, shape and letter recognition, and sound-letter correspondence.

COLOR RECOGNITION

Recognition of colors is a basic readiness skill needed by the young learner. Here are sixteen Silly Scribbles to help reinforce color recognition. There is one Level I and one Level II activity for each of the eight basic colors.

We come in all colors!

SILLY SCRIBBLE TEACHER-DIRECTED PAGE

Level I

COLOR RECOGNITION: red
SILLY SCRIBBLE: wagon
PAPER DIRECTION: "standing up"
STAR COLOR: red

TEACHER DIRECTIONS: Look for the number 1. This will tell you where to make the START line and what color to use.

- Keep in mind the basic strokes described in Section 1.
- Always use the whole paper when doing Silly Scribbles.
- Always write the name of the Silly Scribble or encourage the children to try and write it themselves.
- Emphasize to the children that this is only one way of making a wagon. Discuss other ways.

QUESTIONS YOU COULD ASK:
- Which shape is the biggest?
- How many circles?
- What is in the little red wagon?
- How many whiskers does the animal have?
- Where do you think the animal is going?

ADDITIONAL ACTIVITIES:
- Bring in a real wagon and let the children discuss while touching all of the different shapes that make up a wagon.
- Discuss the kinds of wagons (for example, Conestoga) and uses for a wagon.
- Let's pretend that we are pulling different things in our red wagons, such as a feather, an elephant, a load of eggs. Now let's push it up a steep hill, through a mud puddle, on an icy road.

CREATIVE THINKING STARTERS:
- If you had a magic red wagon and could wish for anything you wanted to be in your wagon, what would it be?
- What would happen if a wagon's wheels were shaped like squares? Triangles? How would this affect the ability to pull it? Ride in it?

SUGGESTED READING:
- *Little Red Wagon Painted Blue* by Robert Hershon. Illustrated by Michaeleen Hershon. Greensboro, NC: Unicorn Press, 1972.

NOTES:

red

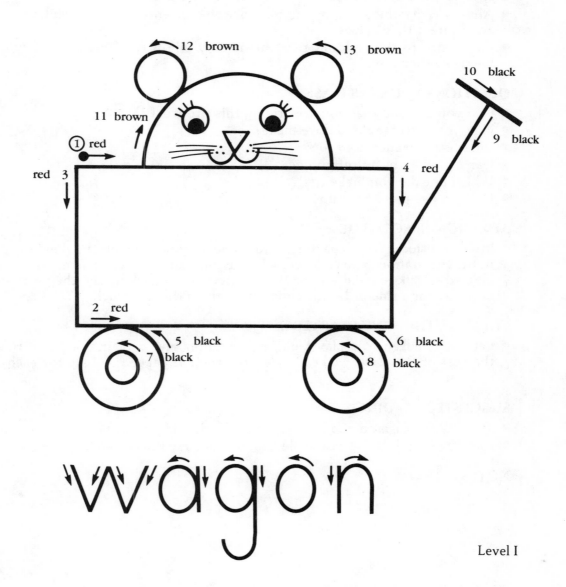

12 brown   13 brown

11 brown

10 black

9 black

① red

red 3

4 red

2 red

5 black

7 black

6 black

8 black

wâgòñ

Level I

SILLY SCRIBBLE TEACHER-DIRECTED PAGE

Level II

COLOR RECOGNITION: red
SILLY SCRIBBLE: fire truck
PAPER DIRECTION: "lying down"
STAR COLOR: red

TEACHER DIRECTIONS: Look for the number 1. This will tell you where to make the START line and what color to use.

- Keep in mind the basic strokes described in Section 1.
- Always use the whole paper when doing Silly Scribbles.
- Always write the name of the Silly Scribble or encourage the children to try and write it themselves.
- Emphasize to the children that this is only one way of making a fire truck. Discuss other ways.

QUESTIONS YOU COULD ASK:
- Can you pretend that you are driving this fire truck?
- How many rectangles did we make?
- What is the ladder used for?
- Can a woman be a firefighter?
- Which line did you make first?
- Did you use more Stan lines or more Carla lines?

ADDITIONAL ACTIVITIES:
- Invite the local fire department to come to your school or take a field trip to the fire station. The children will love this and the fire department is usually pleased to talk to children about fire safety. If you ask nicely, they may either take you for a ride or let the children climb on the fire truck.

CREATIVE THINKING STARTERS:
- Let the children role play being a firefighter and explain good fire rules to the rest of the class. Make simple construction paper fire hats for each child to wear.

SUGGESTED READING:
- *The Little Fire Engine* by Lois Lenski. New York: Henry Z. Walck, 1946.
- *Colors* by John J. Reiss. Scarsdale, NY: Bradbury Press, 1969.

NOTES:

red

fire truck

3 red

12

6 red

red 11 red

red 7

red 5

8

10 black

9 black

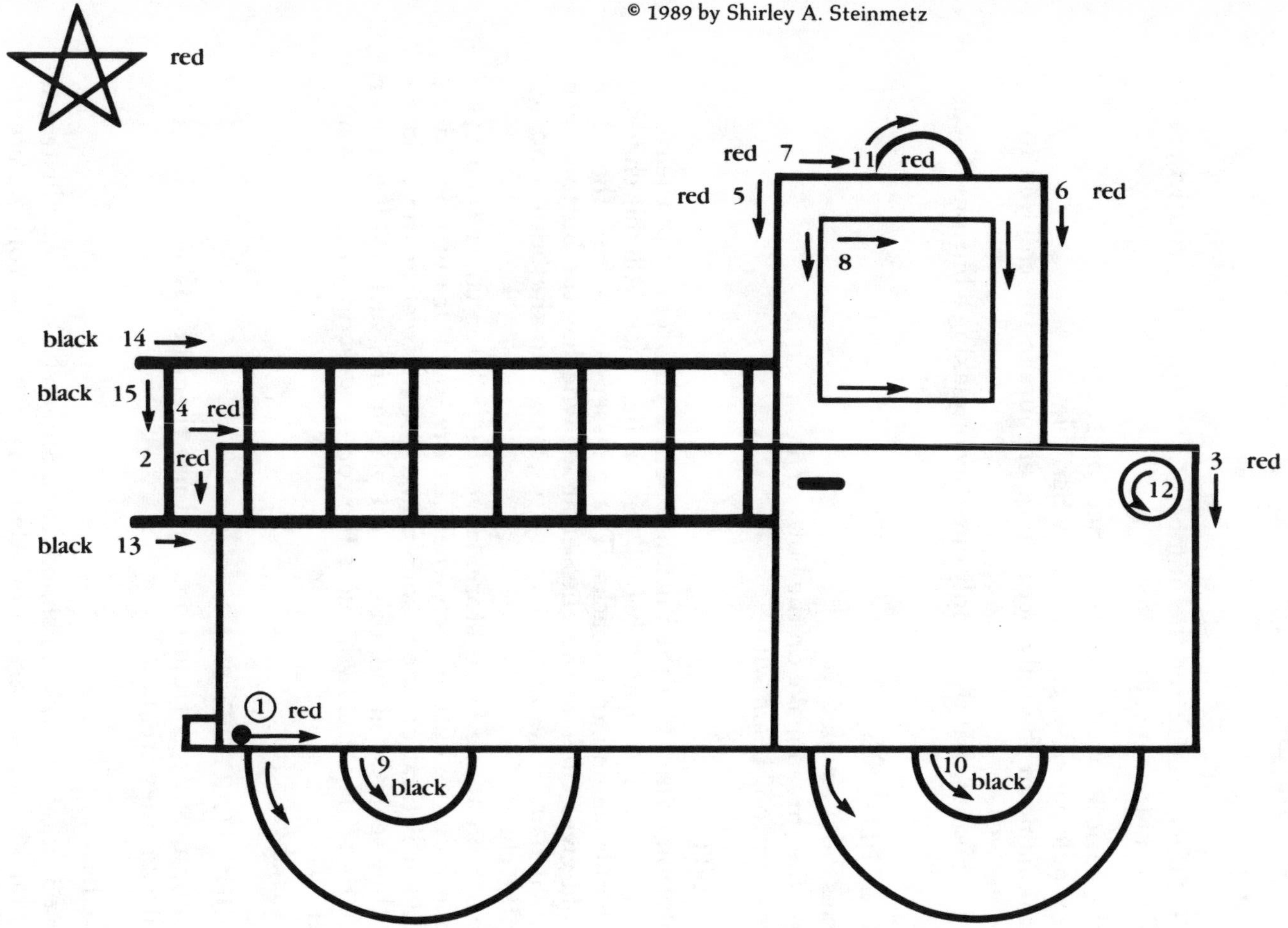

1 red

4 red

2 red

black 14

black 15

black 13

SILLY SCRIBBLE TEACHER-DIRECTED PAGE

Level I

COLOR RECOGNITION: blue
SILLY SCRIBBLE: button
PAPER DIRECTION: "standing up"
STAR COLOR: blue

TEACHER DIRECTIONS: Look for the number 1. This will tell you where to make the START line and what color to use.

- Keep in mind the basic strokes described in Section 1.
- Always use the whole paper when doing Silly Scribbles.
- Always write the name of the Silly Scribble or encourage the children to try and write it themselves.
- Emphasize to the children that this is only one way of making a button. Discuss other ways.

QUESTIONS YOU COULD ASK:
- How many circles did we make?
- What letter does the thread make on the button?
- What letter does "button" begin with?

ADDITIONAL ACTIVITIES:
- Play "Button, Button, Who's Got the Button?" Send a guesser out of the room. Give the button to a child to hold behind his or her back. All the children sit with their hands behind their backs. The guesser comes into the room and another child gives clues to the guesser about who has the button, such as "He has brown hair." The guesser tries to guess who the button holder is by following the clues.
- Find a big blue button at the fabric store. Have the children cover their eyes, then have a child hide the button somewhere in the room. It must be visible; it cannot be hidden behind or under something. Let the rest of the children tell you where they see it by giving the correct placement, such as "It is under the teddy bear's foot." The child who uses the correct description gets to hide the button next.
- Sorting buttons is always fun!

CREATIVE THINKING STARTERS:
- Let children bring in buttons from home and use them in any way they like in a picture or design they create.

SUGGESTED READING:
- *The Land of the Lost Buttons* by Kayako Nishimaki and Shigeo Nakamura. Illustrated by Kayako Nishimaki. English version by Alvin Tresselt. New York: Parents Magazine Press, 1970.

NOTES:

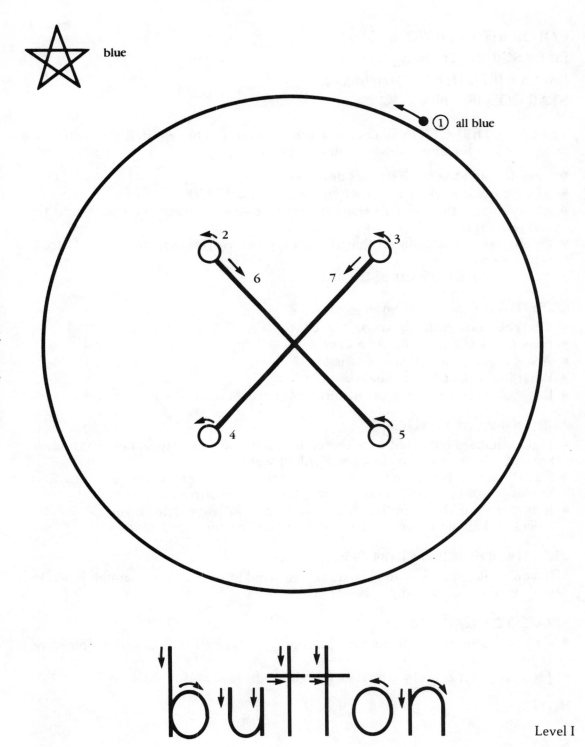

blue

① all blue

2　6　7　3

4　5

button

Level I

SILLY SCRIBBLE TEACHER-DIRECTED PAGE

Level II

COLOR RECOGNITION: blue
SILLY SCRIBBLE: boat
PAPER DIRECTION: "standing up"
STAR COLOR: blue

TEACHER DIRECTIONS: Look for the number 1. This will tell you where to make the START line and what color to use.

- Keep in mind the basic strokes described in Section 1.
- Always use the whole paper when doing Silly Scribbles.
- Always write the name of the Silly Scribble or encourage the children to try and write it themselves.
- Emphasize to the children that this is only one way of making a boat. Discuss other ways.
- Note the different parts of the boat.

QUESTIONS YOU COULD ASK:
- Can you draw yourself sailing this boat?
- How many triangles did we make?
- Are there any curved lines in the boat?
- What letter does "boat" begin with?
- Do you know the names of the different parts of a boat?

ADDITIONAL ACTIVITIES:
- Make small sailboats out of Styrofoam, toothpicks, and paper. Let the children see if the boats will float in a small tub of water.
- Have the children collect or make pictures of different kinds of boats. Sort them according to size, color, or kind. Discuss the differences.
- In a corner of the room let the children make a large sailboat out of wooden blocks and an old sheet. Let the children play, pretend, and dream in it.

CREATIVE THINKING STARTERS:
- If you could sail away in a boat, where would you go? Who would you take with you? What would you need?

SUGGESTED READING:
- *If I Had a Ship* by Ben Schector. Garden City, NY: Doubleday and Company, 1970.
- *The Wreck of the Zephr* by Chris Van Allsburg. Boston: Houghton Mifflin, 1983.

NOTES:

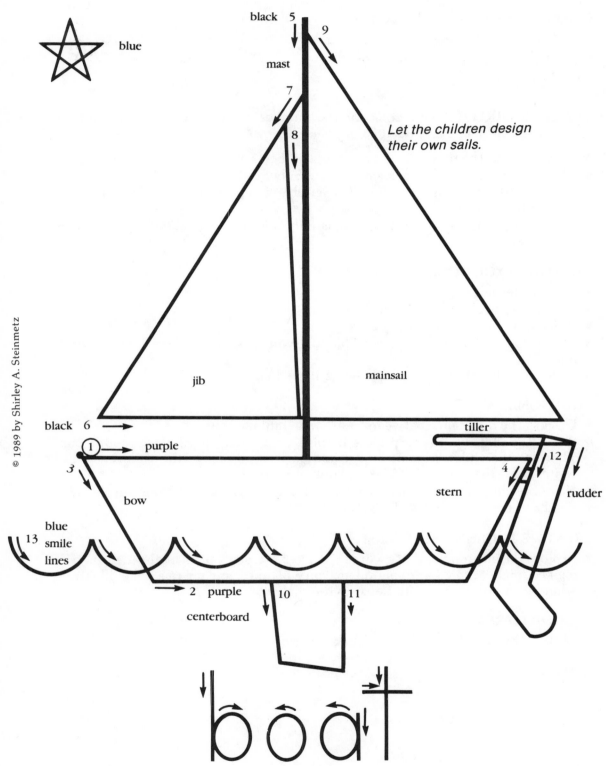

blue

black 5

mast

7

8

9

Let the children design their own sails.

jib

mainsail

black 6

① purple

3

bow

tiller

stern

4

12

rudder

blue smile lines

13

2 purple

centerboard

10

11

boat

© 1989 by Shirley A. Steinmetz

Level II

SILLY SCRIBBLE TEACHER-DIRECTED PAGE

Level I

COLOR RECOGNITION: purple
SILLY SCRIBBLE: pig
PAPER DIRECTION: "lying down"
STAR COLOR: purple

TEACHER DIRECTIONS: Look for the number 1. This will tell you where to make the START line and what color to use.

- Keep in mind the basic strokes described in Section 1.
- Always use the whole paper when doing Silly Scribbles.
- Always write the name of the Silly Scribble or encourage the children to try and write it themselves.
- Emphasize to the children that this is only one way of making a pig. Discuss other ways.

QUESTIONS YOU COULD ASK:
- What letter does "pig" begin with?
- How many ovals did you make?
- What was the first line you made?
- When you look at this Silly Scribble, did you make more Stan lines or Carla lines?
- Is there such a thing as a purple polka-dotted pig?

ADDITIONAL ACTIVITIES:
- Discuss the difference between "real" and "fantasy" pigs.
- Show the children many photos of pigs or a video or filmstrip about pigs. Then let the children paint or cut and paste a pig. Have the children tell or write about their pictures. Make a book of their pictures.
- Have the children count the purple polka dots they made on their purple pig.
- Read and act out *The Three Little Pigs.*

CREATIVE THINKING STARTERS:
- Explore the meaning of these words: piggyback, piggy bank, pigheaded, pigpen, pig bed, pigboat, pig Latin, pigtail, pigs in a blanket, and pig in a poke. Illustrate what you think they mean. Look up the real meanings.

SUGGESTED READING:
- *Small Pig* by Arnold Lobel. New York: Harper & Row, 1969.

NOTES:

© 1989 by Shirley A. Steinmetz

Level I

make purple polka dots

all purple

purple

pig

13

12

10

5

2

3

4

11

9

6

7

8

SILLY SCRIBBLE TEACHER-DIRECTED PAGE

Level II

COLOR RECOGNITION: purple
SILLY SCRIBBLE: porcupine
PAPER DIRECTION: "lying down"
STAR COLOR: purple

TEACHER DIRECTIONS: Look for the number 1. This will tell you where to make the START line and what color to use.

- Keep in mind the basic strokes described in Section 1.
- Always use the whole paper when doing Silly Scribbles.
- Always write the name of the Silly Scribble or encourage the children to try and write it themselves.
- Emphasize to the children that this is only one way of making a porcupine. Discuss other ways.

QUESTIONS YOU COULD ASK:
- What was your first clue about the Silly Scribble?
- Have you ever seen a purple porcupine? Is it real or fantasy?
- What are the quills for?
- What letter does "porcupine" begin with?
- Did you know that baby porcupines are born with quills?

ADDITIONAL ACTIVITIES:
- Using toothpicks for quills and construction paper, let the children glue them onto a paper to make their own porcupine.
- Sort colored quills (toothpicks). Count and see how many of each you have.

CREATIVE THINKING STARTERS:
- How would you hug a porcupine?

SUGGESTED READING:
- *Porcupine's Christmas Blues* by Jane Breskin Zalben. New York: Philomel Books, 1982.
- *Harold and the Purple Crayon* by Crockett Johnson. New York: Harper & Row, 1955.

NOTES:

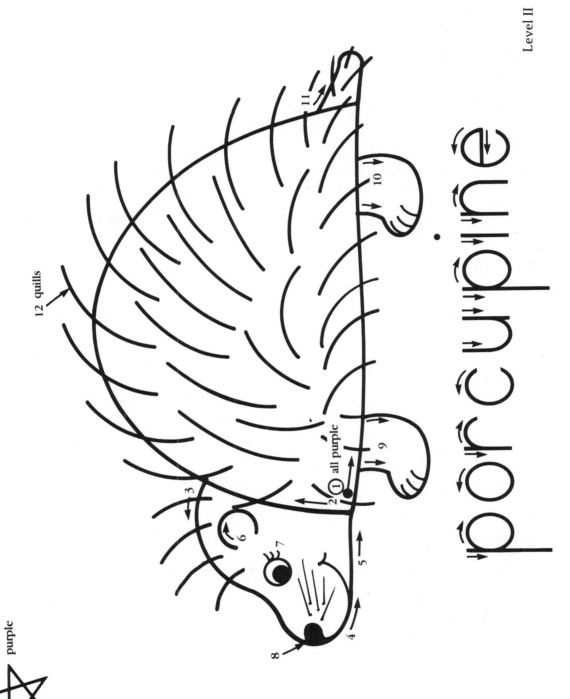

© 1989 by Shirley A. Steinmetz

12 quills

all purple

porcupine

Level II

purple

SILLY SCRIBBLE TEACHER-DIRECTED PAGE

Level I

COLOR RECOGNITION: yellow
SILLY SCRIBBLE: corn
PAPER DIRECTION: "lying down"
STAR COLOR: yellow

TEACHER DIRECTIONS: Look for the number 1. This will tell you where to make the START line and what color to use.

- Keep in mind the basic strokes described in Section 1.
- Always use the whole paper when doing Silly Scribbles.
- Always write the name of the Silly Scribble or encourage the children to try and write it themselves.
- Emphasize to the children that this is only one way of making a corn cob. Discuss other ways.

QUESTIONS YOU COULD ASK:

- Why do you think we are using a yellow "c" to make corn?
- How many yellow corn "c's" did you make?
- Do you know what the vegetable is called when you eat a whole ear of corn? (corn on the cob).

ADDITIONAL ACTIVITIES:

- Using examples of field corn, popcorn, and Indian corn, discuss the differences.
- Sort a bowl of different kinds of corn into small individual bowls.
- Make popcorn as a snack or have corn on the cob.
- Try and grow some corn if you have a sunny window.
- Make cornbread and serve as a snack with butter.
- How many products can you think of that have corn in them? (corn flakes, corn chips).

CREATIVE THINKING STARTERS:

- Does every cob of corn have the same amount of rows? How can you find out?
- Compare the Silly Scribble corn picture with an actual ear of corn. In what ways are they alike? Different?

SUGGESTED READING:

- *The Popcorn Dragon* by Jane Thayer. Illustrated by Jay Hyde Barnum. New York: William Morrow and Company, 1953.

NOTES:

yellow ①

2 green →

green 3

green 4

fill in with yellow "C's"

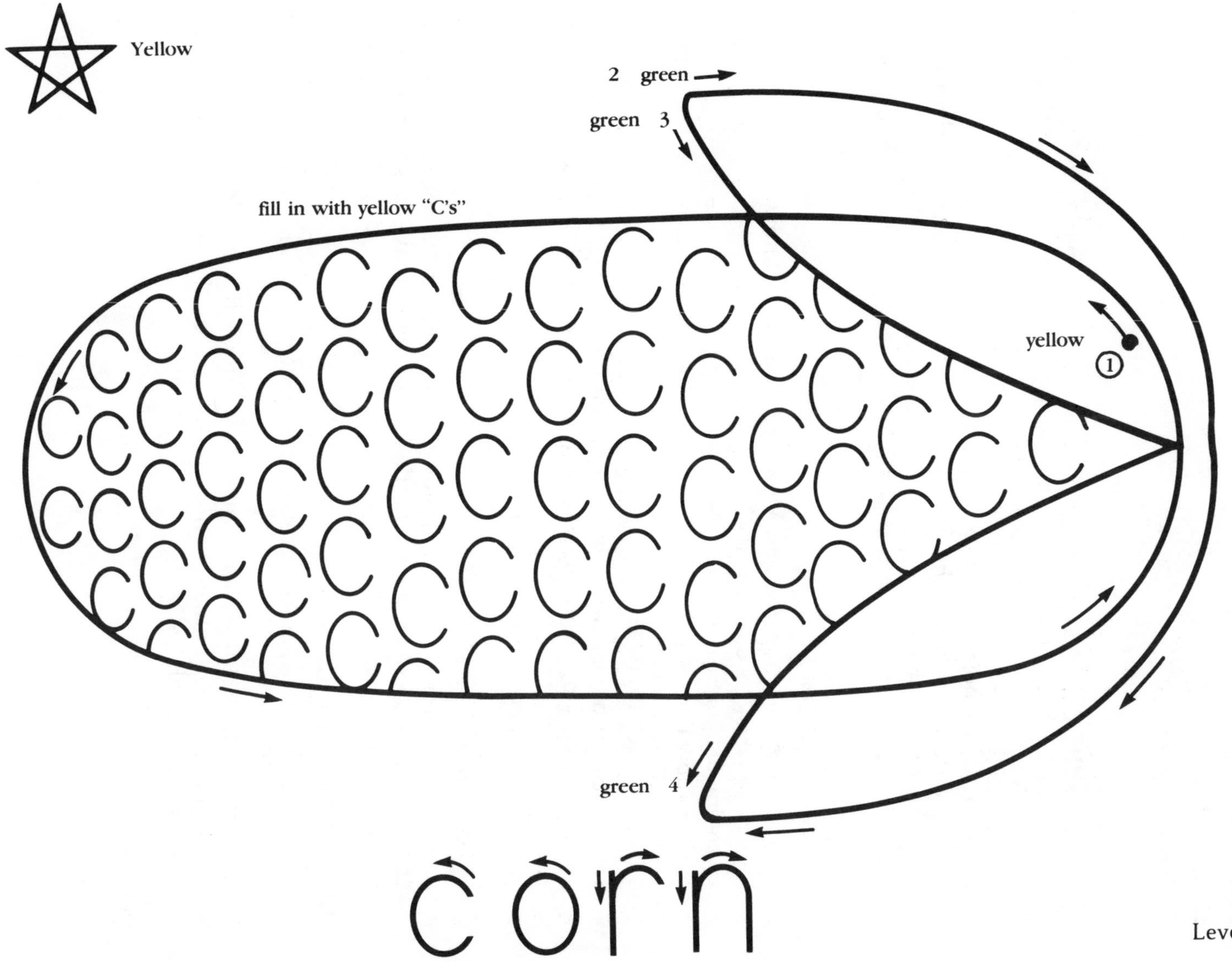

Yellow

córn

SILLY SCRIBBLE TEACHER-DIRECTED PAGE

Level II

COLOR RECOGNITION: yellow
SILLY SCRIBBLE: lion
PAPER DIRECTION: "standing up"
STAR COLOR: yellow

TEACHER DIRECTIONS: Look for the number 1. This will tell you where to make the START line and what color to use.

- Keep in mind the basic strokes described in Section 1.
- Always use the whole paper when doing Silly Scribbles.
- Always write the name of the Silly Scribble or encourage the children to try and write it themselves.
- Emphasize to the children that this is only one way of making a lion. Discuss other ways.

QUESTIONS YOU COULD ASK:

- Is the lion we made a Daddy or a Mommy? How do we know?
- How many whiskers did we make?
- Which line did you make first?
- Did you know lions say "hello" to each other by rubbing faces with each other?

ADDITIONAL ACTIVITIES:

- Pretend you are a lion. How would you sound?
- If you were walking in the jungle, how would you walk if you were a lion? Would I hear you?
- Play "We're Going on a Lion Hunt."

CREATIVE THINKING STARTERS:

- Discuss the difference between the lion and the mouse in the suggested reading. Which would you rather be? Why? (Be certain not to make judgments; accept all responses as equally valid.)

SUGGESTED READING:

- *The Lion and the Mouse* by Aesop. Illustrated by Bob Dole. Mahwah, NJ: Troll Associates, 1981.
- *Lambert the Sheepish Lion* by Walt Disney. New York: Random House, 1977.
- *The Happy Lion* by Louise Fatio. Illustrated by Roger Duvoisin. New York: McGraw-Hill, 1954.

NOTES:

yellow

13   yellow and brown mane

all yellow

black

10

1

9

11

2

3

7

12

8

4

5

6

lion

Level II

SILLY SCRIBBLE TEACHER-DIRECTED PAGE

Level I

COLOR RECOGNITION: green
SILLY SCRIBBLE: watermelon
PAPER DIRECTION: "lying down"
STAR COLOR: green

TEACHER DIRECTIONS: Look for the number 1. This will tell you where to make the START line and what color to use.

- Keep in mind the basic strokes described in Section 1.
- Always use the whole paper when doing Silly Scribbles.
- Always write the name of the Silly Scribble or encourage the children to try and write it themselves.
- Emphasize to the children that this is only one way of making a watermelon. Discuss other ways.

QUESTIONS YOU COULD ASK:
- How many seeds did we make?
- What part of the watermelon do you eat?
- Can you think of any other watermelon-flavored items you have eaten? (Candy, gum)
- Why do you like (or not like) to eat watermelon?

ADDITIONAL ACTIVITIES:
- Serve watermelon as a snack.
- Discuss different fruits. Is watermelon the biggest? Which is the smallest when it's full grown?
- Since a watermelon's weight is mostly water (over 90 percent), discuss water and what we need it for. What are all the things we do using water?

CREATIVE THINKING STARTERS:
- Do you know how to tell if a watermelon is ripe enough to eat? Bring in two watermelons and let the children experiment and make predictions on which is ripe.
- How do you think the watermelon got its name?

SUGGESTED READING:
- *Is It Red? Is It Yellow? Is It Blue?* by Tana Hoban. New York: Greenwillow Books, 1978.

NOTES:

green

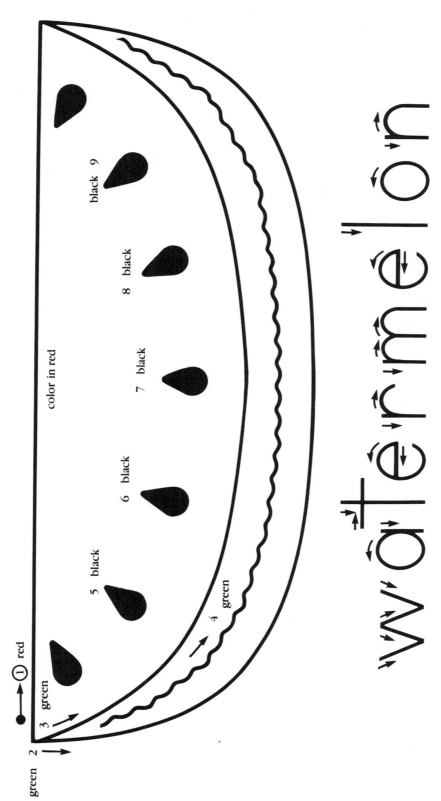

green 2

3 green

① red

color in red

5 black

6 black

7 black

8 black

black 9

4 green

watermelon

SILLY SCRIBBLE TEACHER-DIRECTED PAGE

Level II

COLOR RECOGNITION: green

SILLY SCRIBBLE: turtle

PAPER DIRECTION: "lying down"

STAR COLOR: green

TEACHER DIRECTIONS: Look for the number 1. This will tell you where to make the START line and what color to use.

- Keep in mind the basic strokes described in Section 1.
- Always use the whole paper when doing Silly Scribbles.
- Always write the name of the Silly Scribble or encourage the children to try and write it themselves.
- Emphasize to the children that this is only one way of making a turtle. Discuss other ways.

QUESTIONS YOU COULD ASK:

- What letter does "turtle" begin with?
- Why do we see only two feet? Doesn't a turtle have four?
- Did you know that the only reptile that has a shell is the turtle?
- Where do you think this turtle lives? In a pond? In a backyard? In a forest? Draw it on the paper.

ADDITIONAL ACTIVITIES:

- Read and do the fingerplay *Little Turtle* by Vachel Lindsay.
- Pretend you are a turtle and pull yourself into your shell. Slowly come out of your shell. Oops! Here comes a dog! What will you do? Here comes a fly! Now what will you do?

CREATIVE THINKING STARTERS:

- Draw a picture of what you think a turtle would look like without its shell.

SUGGESTED READING:

- *Little Turtle's Big Adventure* by David Harrison. Illustrated by J. P. Miller. New York: Random House, 1967, 1978.

NOTES:

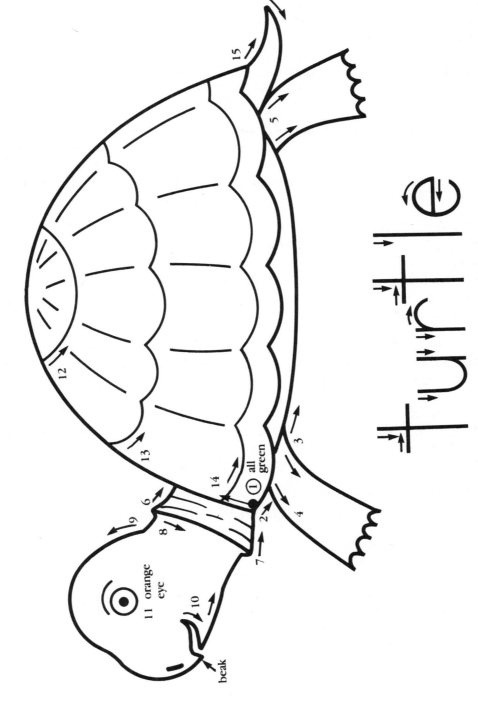

© 1989 by Shirley A. Steinmetz

green

Level II

turtle

SILLY SCRIBBLE TEACHER-DIRECTED PAGE

Level I

COLOR RECOGNITION: orange
SILLY SCRIBBLE: jack-o'-lantern
PAPER DIRECTION: "standing up"
STAR COLOR: orange

TEACHER DIRECTIONS: Look for the number 1. This will tell you where to make the START line and what color to use.

- Keep in mind the basic strokes described in Section 1.
- Always use the whole paper when doing Silly Scribbles.
- Always write the name of the Silly Scribble or encourage the children to try and write it themselves.
- Emphasize to the children that this is only one way of making a jack-o'-lantern face. Discuss other ways.

QUESTIONS YOU COULD ASK:
- What shape are the eyes? How many circles?
- What shape is the nose?
- Why do you think we colored the inside of the face yellow?
- You may want to discuss the different shapes to make a face. Can the children make their own face on the pumpkin?

ADDITIONAL ACTIVITIES:
- Take a pumpkin and turn it into a jack-o'-lantern by cutting out a face.
- Take a trip to a pumpkin patch and see how pumpkins grow.
- Explore and discuss the difference between the inside and the outside of a pumpkin.
- Use the seeds and let the children paste them on paper in sets of different numbers.
- Cook the pumpkin seeds and eat as a snack.

CREATIVE THINKING STARTERS:
- What else could you use a hollowed-out pumpkin for?

SUGGESTED READING:
- *A Mother Goose A B C in a Pumpkin Shell* by Joan Walsh Anglund. New York: Harcourt, Brace and World, 1960.
- *The Pumpkin Patch* by Patricia Miles Martin. Illustrated by Tom Hamil. New York: G. P. Putnam, 1966.

NOTES:

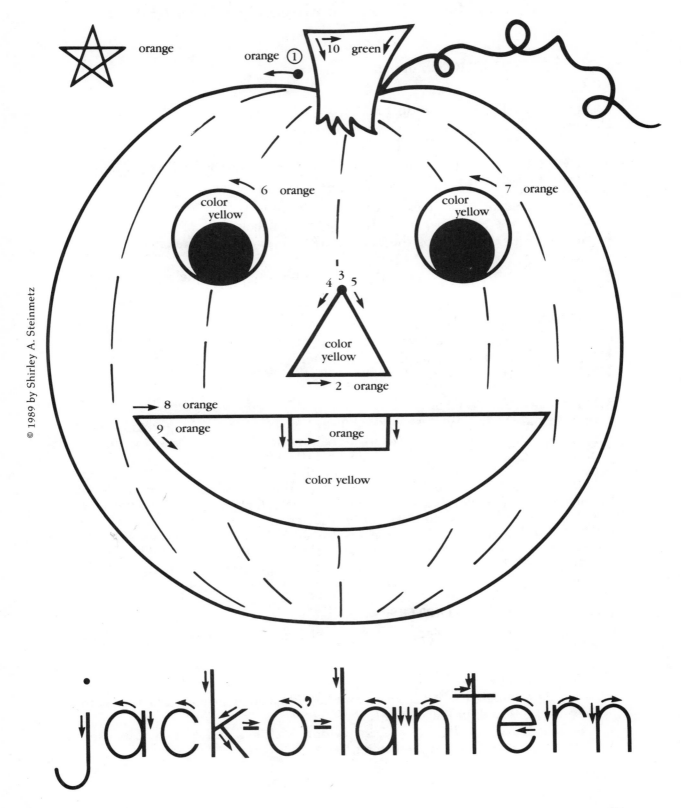

orange

orange ① →10 green

orange 6

orange 7

color yellow

color yellow

4 3 5

color yellow

2 orange

8 orange

9 orange

orange

color yellow

jack-o'-lantern

Level I

SILLY SCRIBBLE TEACHER-DIRECTED PAGE

Level II

COLOR RECOGNITION: orange
SILLY SCRIBBLE: tiger
PAPER DIRECTION: "standing up"
STAR COLOR: orange

TEACHER DIRECTIONS: Look for the number 1. This will tell you where to make the START line and what color to use.

- Keep in mind the basic strokes described in Section 1.
- Always use the whole paper when doing Silly Scribbles.
- Always write the name of the Silly Scribble or encourage the children to try and write it themselves.
- Emphasize to the children that this is only one way of making a tiger. Discuss other ways.

QUESTIONS YOU COULD ASK:

- What was your first clue that this was a tiger?
- How many whiskers did we make altogether?
- Why do you think this tiger is smiling?

ADDITIONAL ACTIVITIES:

- Play "Tiger, Tiger, Who Has Your Tail?" Make a pretend tiger tail out of paper or fabric. One child sits in a chair with his or her back to the rest of the children. (This child is sitting a little bit on the tail so that it may be easily removed without tearing.) The child who sneaks up to remove the tail sits with the rest of the children with the tail behind his or her back. The rest of the children also have their hands behind their backs, pretending to have the tail. When they are ready, they chant "Tiger, tiger, who has your tail?" The "tiger" gets three guesses to see if he or she can find out who has the tail. If the "tiger" gets tricked, the new "tiger" (the child with the tail) is it. If the child guesses correctly, he or she gets another turn as the "tiger."

CREATIVE THINKING STARTERS:

- Do you think a tiger is black with orange stripes, or orange with black stripes? Why?

SUGGESTED READING:

- *Half-as-Big and the Tiger* by Bernice Frankel. Illustrated by Leonard Weisgard. New York: Franklin Watts, 1961.
- *Who Ever Heard of a Tiger in a Tree* by John McInnes and Rosalie Davidson. Champaign, IL: Garrard Publishing, 1971.

NOTES:

orange

with black stripes

black
19

all orange

© 1989 by Shirley A. Steinmetz

tiger

Level II

SILLY SCRIBBLE TEACHER-DIRECTED PAGE

Level I

COLOR RECOGNITION: brown
SILLY SCRIBBLE: bear (teddy)
PAPER DIRECTION: "standing up"
STAR COLOR: brown

TEACHER DIRECTIONS: Look for the number 1. This will tell you where to make the START line and what color to use.

- Keep in mind the basic strokes described in Section 1.
- Always use the whole paper when doing Silly Scribbles.
- Always write the name of the Silly Scribble or encourage the children to try and write it themselves.
- Emphasize to the children that this is only one way of making a teddy bear. Discuss other ways.

QUESTIONS YOU COULD ASK:
- How many circles did we use?
- How many eyelashes did we make altogether?
- What shape is the bear's nose?
- What sound does the word "bear" end with?
- Did you know the toymakers started making stuffed bears after a cartoon was published showing President Teddy Roosevelt holding a bear cub?

ADDITIONAL ACTIVITIES:
- Invite the children to bring in their favorite teddy bear or stuffed toy. Encourage the children to tell each bear's size, color, and name. After sharing the bears, sort them according to size or color.

CREATIVE THINKING STARTERS:
- If you could make your teddy bear real, what would you do with it?

SUGGESTED READING:
- *Corduroy* by Don Freeman. New York: The Viking Press, 1968.
- *Brown Bear, Brown Bear, What Do You See?* by Bill Martin, Jr. with pictures by Eric Carle. Toronto: Holt, Rinehart and Winston of Canada, 1970.

NOTES:

brown

all brown
①

9

10

11

12

3 2

4

red 13 red

red   red

5

6

7   8

bear

Level I

SILLY SCRIBBLE TEACHER-DIRECTED PAGE

COLOR RECOGNITION: brown
SILLY SCRIBBLE: squirrel
PAPER DIRECTION: "standing up"
STAR COLOR: brown

TEACHER DIRECTIONS: Look for the number 1. This will tell you where to make the START line and what color to use.

- Keep in mind the basic strokes described in Section 1.
- Always use the whole paper when doing Silly Scribbles.
- Always write the name of the Silly Scribble or encourage the children to try and write it themselves.
- Emphasize to the children that this is only one way of making a squirrel. Discuss other ways.

QUESTIONS YOU COULD ASK:
- How many circles did we use?
- What is the squirrel going to do with the acorn?
- Did you know that the squirrel uses its tail for balance, an umbrella, a blanket in cold weather, and for shade in warm weather?

ADDITIONAL ACTIVITIES:
- Play "Squirrels and Trees." Pair two children and have them face each other and hold hands. They will be the tree. Put one other child between them as the squirrel. Plan to have one or two leftover "squirrels" so there will always be more squirrels than trees to hide in. Explain that the odd child out will say, "Find a new tree!" They must run to a "new" tree without bumping into each other. Try to give each child a chance to be a squirrel.

CREATIVE THINKING STARTERS:
- Pretend you are a squirrel. Design a tree house for your home. What would it look like? What would be in your home?

SUGGESTED READING:
- *Merle the High Flying Squirrel* by Bill Peet. Boston: Houghton Mifflin, 1974.
- *The Meanest Squirrel I Ever Met* by Gene Zion. Illustrated by Margaret Bloy Graham. New York: Charles Scribner's Sons, 1962.

NOTES:

brown

all brown
①

black

green

squirrel

Level II

SILLY SCRIBBLE TEACHER-DIRECTED PAGE

Level I

COLOR RECOGNITION: black
SILLY SCRIBBLE: bat
PAPER DIRECTION: "lying down"
STAR COLOR: black

TEACHER DIRECTIONS: Look for the number 1. This will tell you where to make the START line and what color to use.

- Keep in mind the basic strokes described in Section 1.
- Always use the whole paper when doing Silly Scribbles.
- Always write the name of the Silly Scribble or encourage the children to try and write it themselves.
- Emphasize to the children that this is only one way of making a bat. Discuss other ways.

QUESTIONS YOU COULD ASK:

- What letter does "bat" begin with?
- How many eyelashes did we make on each eye?
- Do bats come in any color other than black?
- Did you know that a bat is a mammal and the only one that flies?

ADDITIONAL ACTIVITIES:

- If you have ever watched *Sesame Street* you will know that the Count has bats for pets. Have the children make ten different bats and number them 1 through 10. Have the children count them. Then have one fly away and see how many are left until you reach zero.

CREATIVE THINKING STARTERS:

- Turn out the lights in your room and have the children pretend they are bats flying around the room. Oh, here comes the sun . . . fly back to the cave and wrap up to go to sleep. (Since you cannot hang upside-down, have the children lie down and wrap up in their "wings" to go to sleep.)

SUGGESTED READING:

- *Hattie, the Backstage Bat* by Don Freeman. New York: The Viking Press, 1970.
- *Lavinia Bat* by Russel Hoban. Illustrated by Martin Baynton. New York: Holt, Rinehart and Winston, 1984.

NOTES:

Level I

second finger

third finger

fourth finger

thumb

fifth finger

3

6

2

all black ①

8

7

frown lines

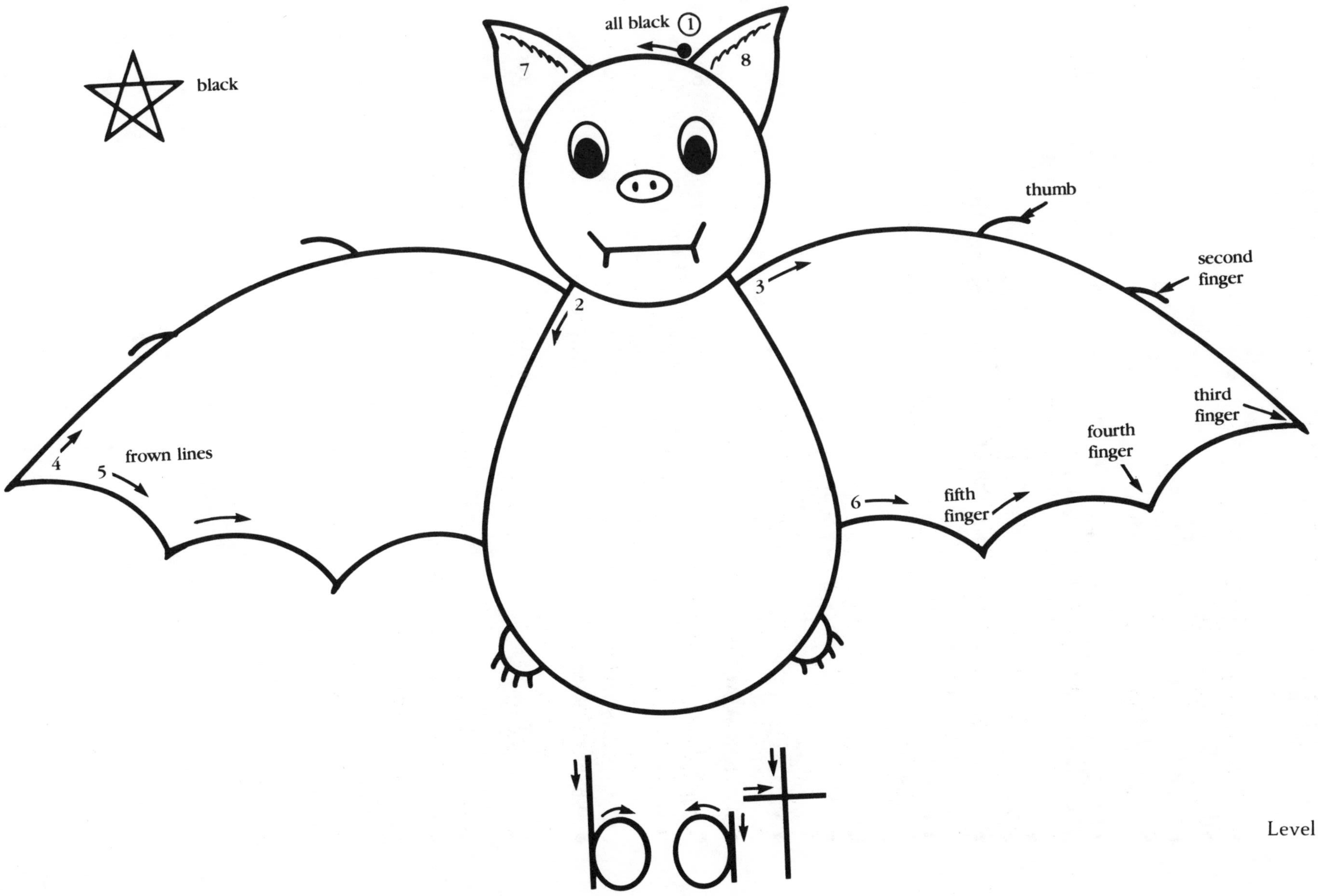

5

4

black

bat

SILLY SCRIBBLE TEACHER-DIRECTED PAGE

Level II

COLOR RECOGNITION: black
SILLY SCRIBBLE: witch
PAPER DIRECTION: "standing up"
STAR COLOR: black

TEACHER DIRECTIONS: Look for the number 1. This will tell you where to make the START line and what color to use.

- Keep in mind the basic strokes described in Section 1.
- Always use the whole paper when doing Silly Scribbles.
- Always write the name of the Silly Scribble or encourage the children to try and write it themselves.
- Emphasize to the children that this is only one way of making a witch. Discuss other ways.

QUESTIONS YOU COULD ASK:

- What letter does "witch" begin with?
- How many stripes did we put on her socks?
- What is the pattern of the stripes?

ADDITIONAL ACTIVITIES:

- Let's pretend that we are witches and we are brewing some magic potion. What would we put into our magic pot? Make a list of the secret ingredients. What will this magic potion do?

CREATIVE THINKING STARTERS:

- What is a witch? Are there boy witches? Why would a person want to be a witch?
- Pretend you are a witch riding on your broom. Can you fly around the room on your broom?

SUGGESTED READING:

- *Humbug Witch* by Lorna Balian. Nashville: Abingdon Press, 1983.

NOTES:

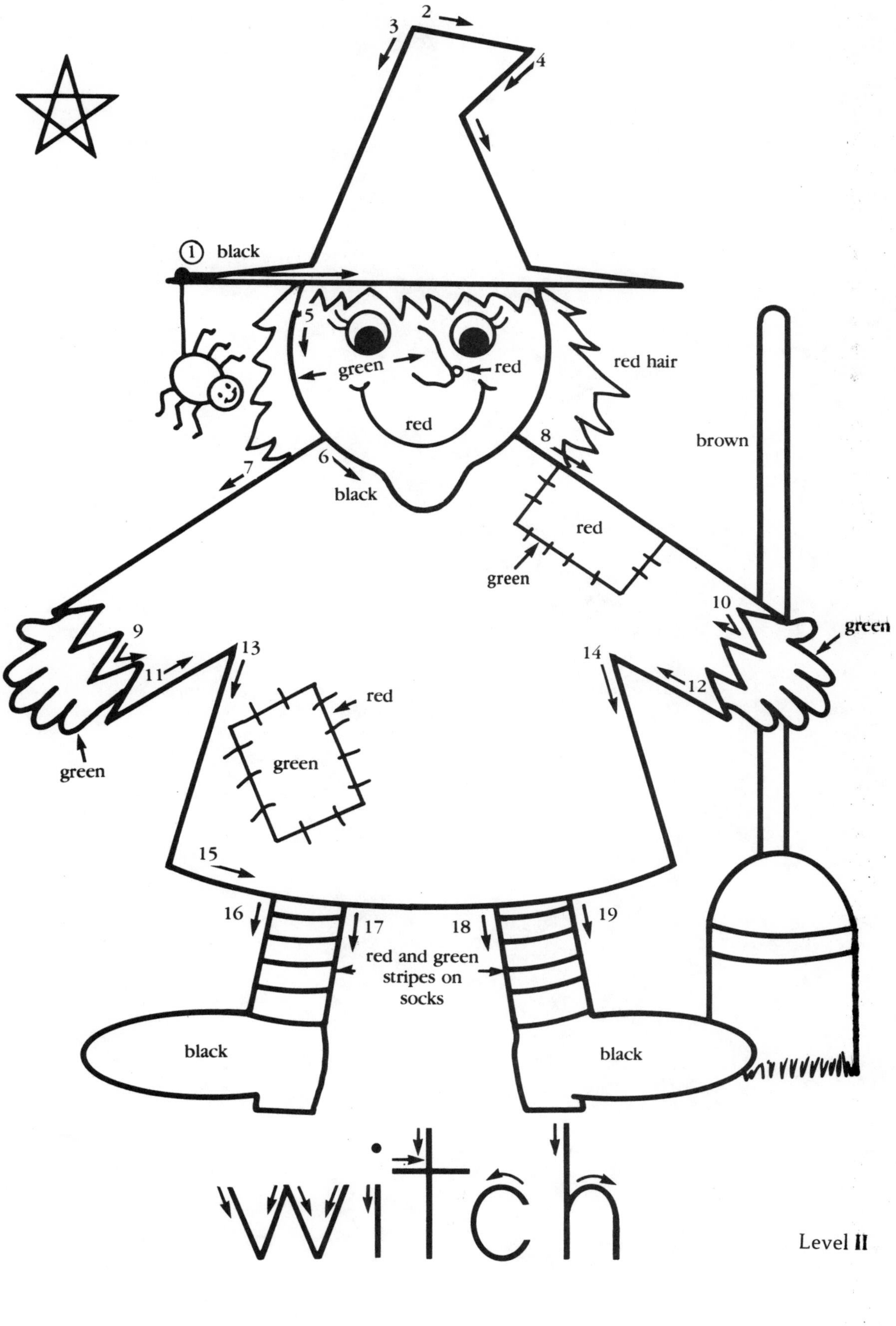

① black

3

2

4

green — red

red

red hair

brown

black

8

red

green

7

6

black

9

11

13

red

green

10

green

14

12

green

15

16   17   18   19

red and green stripes on socks

black

black

witch

Level II

© 1989 by Shirley A. Steinmetz

SHAPE RECOGNITION

There are two shapes that Carla makes: a circle and an oval. Stan makes three shapes: a rectangle, a square, and a triangle. Here you will find one Silly Scribble for each shape listed. These Silly Scribbles are all on Level I. You can reinforce recognition of shapes whenever you do a Silly Scribble by asking the children to name what shapes have been made.

circle ball (Level I) • 52

oval fish (Level I) • 54

square robot (Level I) • 56

rectangle aquarium (Level I) • 58

triangle tepee (Level I) • 60

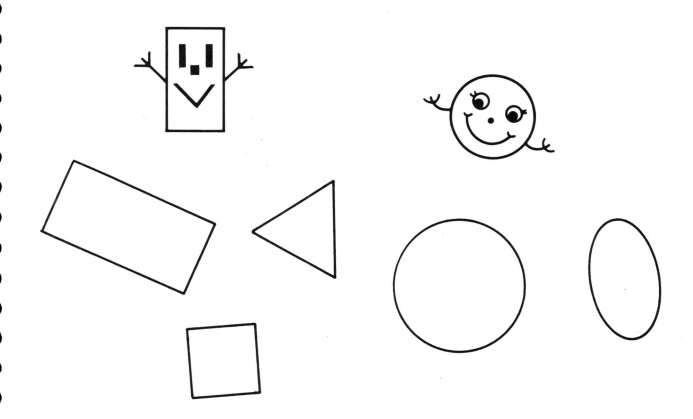

SILLY SCRIBBLE TEACHER-DIRECTED PAGE

Level I

SHAPE RECOGNITION: circle
SILLY SCRIBBLE: ball
PAPER DIRECTION: "standing up"
STAR COLOR: blue

TEACHER DIRECTIONS: Look for the number 1. This will tell you where to make the START line and what color to use.

- Keep in mind the basic strokes described in Section 1.
- Always use the whole paper when doing Silly Scribbles.
- Always write the name of the Silly Scribble or encourage the children to try and write it themselves.
- Emphasize to the children that this is only one way of making a ball. Discuss other ways.

QUESTIONS YOU COULD ASK:
- What shape is this ball?
- Are all balls shaped like this one?
- What letter does "ball" begin with?
- What is your favorite game played with a ball?

ADDITIONAL ACTIVITIES:
- Practice rolling, tossing, and catching a ball with a friend.
- Can you count how many times you can bounce a ball?
- Make a list of all the games you can think of that are played with a ball. Draw a picture of each ball.
- Get a selection of many different kinds of balls and sort them by size or color.

CREATIVE THINKING STARTERS:
- Pretend you are a ball. First, I have to fill you up with air. Now you are bouncing . . . rolling . . . being sat on by an elephant! You popped!

SUGGESTED READING:
- *Shapes, Shapes, Shapes* by Tana Hoban. New York: Greenwillow Books, 1986.

NOTES:

blue

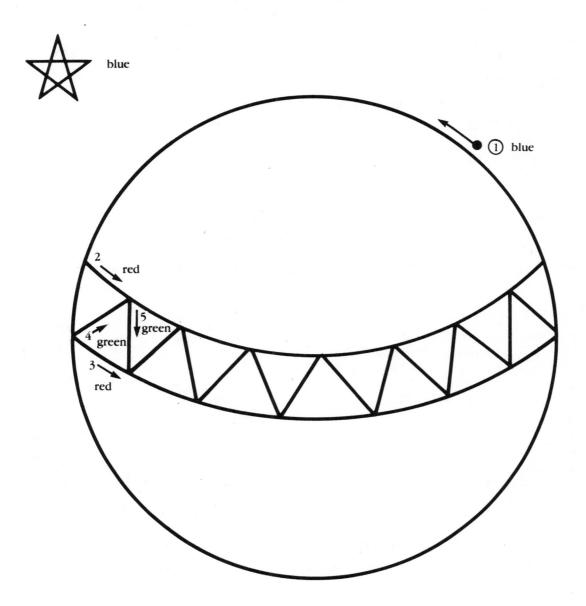

2 red

5 green

4 green

3 red

① blue

ball

Level I

SILLY SCRIBBLE TEACHER-DIRECTED PAGE

Level I

SHAPE RECOGNITION: oval
SILLY SCRIBBLE: fish
PAPER DIRECTION: "lying down"
STAR COLOR: orange

TEACHER DIRECTIONS: Look for the number 1. This will tell you where to make the START line and what color to use.

* Keep in mind the basic strokes described in Section 1.
* Always use the whole paper when doing Silly Scribbles.
* Always write the name of the Silly Scribble or encourage the children to try and write it themselves.
* Emphasize to the children that this is only one way of making a fish. Discuss other ways.

QUESTIONS YOU COULD ASK:
* What shape is the body of the fish?
* Do you know which part is the fin? Tail?
* What letter does "fish" begin with?

ADDITIONAL ACTIVITIES:
* Have the children make ten little fish with numbers 1 through 10 on them. Help the children make a small fishing pole with a magnet. You can use a pencil or stick. Hook a paper clip to each fish and let the children go fishing. See if they can catch the fish in order and count them. Take one away and then count how many are left to zero. Let the children take their fish home in a folded, blue piece of paper.
* Buy a goldfish for the class to watch and enjoy. Assign a daily fish feeder.

CREATIVE THINKING STARTERS:
* Pretend you are a fish swimming in the ocean. Oh my, here comes a shark! Quick, hide!

SUGGESTED READING:
* *Fish Is Fish* by Leo Lionni. New York: Random House, 1970.
* *My Goldfish* by Herbert H. Wong and Matthew F. Vessel. Illustrated by Arvis L. Stewart. Reading, MA: Addison-Wesley, 1969.

NOTES:

Level I

© 1989 by Shirley A. Steinmetz

fish

all purple

orange

orange eye

1

2

3

4

5

6

7

8

9

10

11

12

16 green

15 green

13 brown

14 blue smile lines

orange

SILLY SCRIBBLE TEACHER-DIRECTED PAGE

Level I

SHAPE RECOGNITION: square
SILLY SCRIBBLE: robot
PAPER DIRECTION: "standing up"
STAR COLOR: blue

TEACHER DIRECTIONS: Look for the number 1. This will tell you where to make the START line and what color to use.

- Keep in mind the basic strokes described in Section 1.
- Always use the whole paper when doing Silly Scribbles.
- Always write the name of the Silly Scribble or encourage the children to try and write it themselves.
- Emphasize to the children that this is only one way of making a robot. Discuss other ways.

QUESTIONS YOU COULD ASK:

- Let the children make their own faces for the robot. What are some of the differences?
- How many squares did we need to make our robot?
- Which one is the biggest? Smallest?
- How many rectangles? Circles?
- Who remembers which shape we made first?
- What do you notice about the robot's buttons?

ADDITIONAL ACTIVITIES:

- Pretend you are a robot, and I have just turned you on. How would you move? What would happen if your battery ran down?
- Have the children trace around different shapes to cut and paste together their own robot. Discuss the endless possibilities.

CREATIVE THINKING STARTERS:

- Why are the robot's joints round? Discuss ball and socket.
- Could you draw a picture and then write about your favorite part of a movie that involved a robot?

SUGGESTED READING:

- *Applebaums Have a Robot* by Jane Thayer. Illustrated by Bari Weissman. New York: William Morrow, 1980.
- *The Laziest Robot in Zone One* by Lillian and Phoebe Hoban. Illustrated by Lillian Hoban. New York: Harper & Row, 1983.

NOTES:

blue

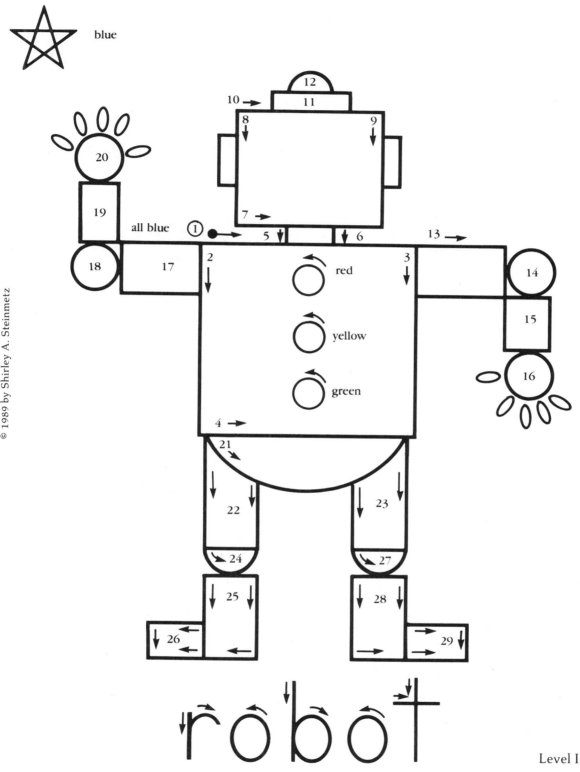

all blue

12
11
10 →
8
9
7 →
1 • →
5
6
13 →
2
red
3
yellow
green
14
15
16
18
17
19
20
4 →
21
22
23
24
27
25
28
26
29

© 1989 by Shirley A. Steinmetz

robot

Level I

SILLY SCRIBBLE TEACHER-DIRECTED PAGE

Level I

SHAPE RECOGNITION: rectangle
SILLY SCRIBBLE: aquarium
PAPER DIRECTION: "lying down"
STAR COLOR: orange

TEACHER DIRECTIONS: Look for the number 1. This will tell you where to make the START line and what color to use.

- Keep in mind the basic strokes described in Section 1.
- Always use the whole paper when doing Silly Scribbles.
- Always write the name of the Silly Scribble or encourage the children to try and write it themselves.
- Emphasize to the children that this is only one way of making an aquarium. Discuss other ways.

QUESTIONS YOU COULD ASK:
- What goes into an aquarium?
- Can you make some fish in the aquarium?
- What sound does "aquarium" begin with?

ADDITIONAL ACTIVITIES:
- Visit a nearby aquarium if possible.
- Let each child cut and paste fish out of scrap paper and paste them onto a sheet of blue paper to make an aquarium.
- Have the children tell about any aquariums they have had at home. Make a list of the different kinds of fish they have had.
- Start an aquarium in your room.

CREATIVE THINKING STARTERS:
- Pretend you are a fish and design an aquarium for yourself. Don't forget a bed, toys, and a television set!

SUGGESTED READING:
- *Aquariums & Terrariums* by Ray Broekel. Chicago: Children's Press, 1982.
- *Tropical Fish* by Ray Broekel. Chicago: Children's Press, 1983.
- *Marigold the Goldfish* by Margaret Sanford Pursell. Minneapolis: Carolrhoda Books, 1976.

NOTES:

Level I

aquarium

orange

blue

green

green

red

red

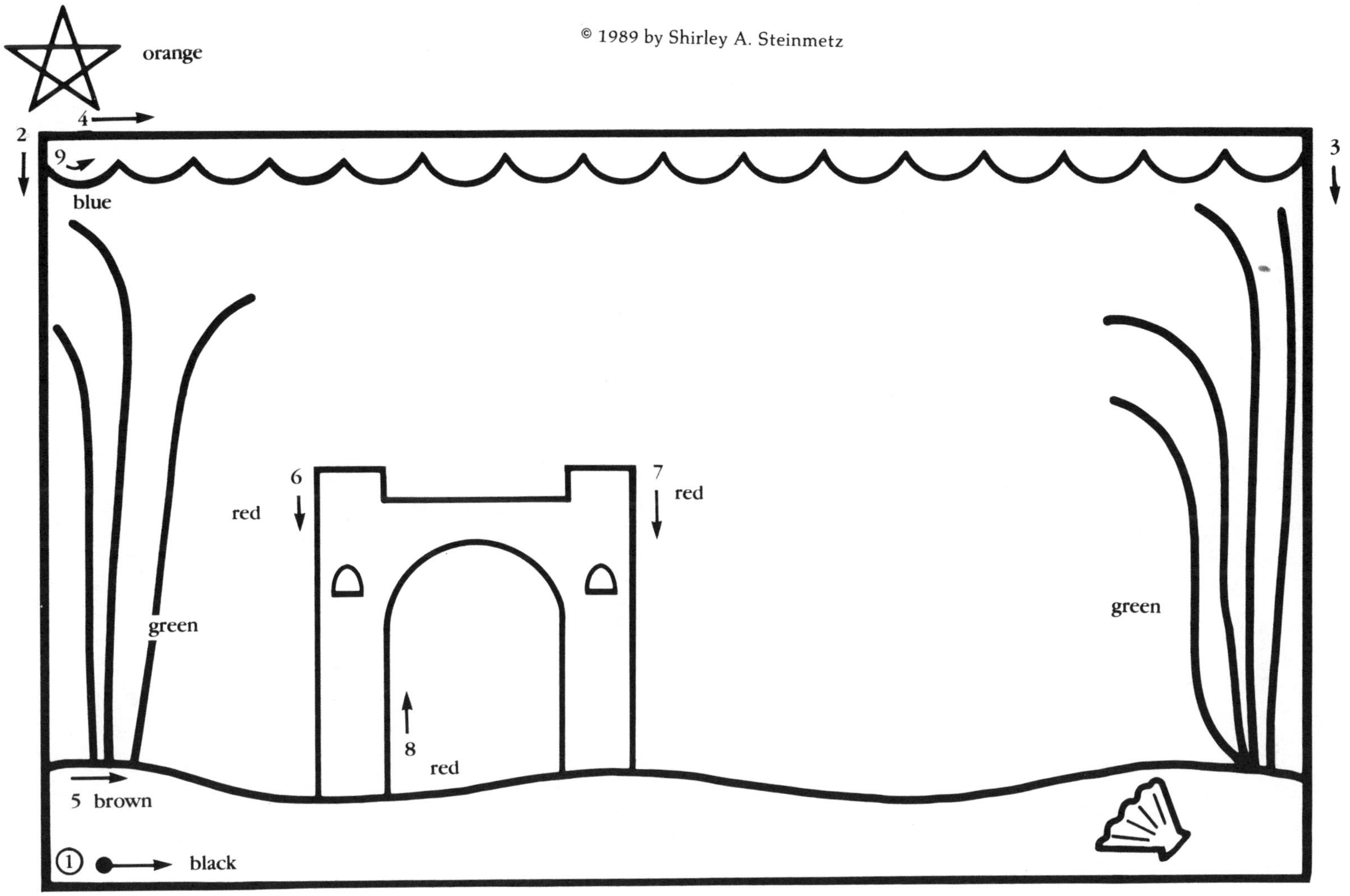

red

brown

black

2

3

4

5

6

7

8

9

1

SILLY SCRIBBLE TEACHER-DIRECTED PAGE

Level I

SHAPE RECOGNITION: triangle
SILLY SCRIBBLE: tepee
PAPER DIRECTION: "standing up"
STAR COLOR: green

TEACHER DIRECTIONS: Look for the number 1. This will tell you where to make the START line and what color to use.

- Keep in mind the basic strokes described in Section 1.
- Always use the whole paper when doing Silly Scribbles.
- Always write the name of the Silly Scribble or encourage the children to try and write it themselves.
- Emphasize to the children that this is only one way of making a tepee. Discuss other ways.

QUESTIONS YOU COULD ASK:

- What shape is the tepee?
- What do the pictures of the sun mean?
- What story might the canoe and spear tell? Make up two or three stories together.

ADDITIONAL ACTIVITIES:

- After reading some books on Indians, let the children make up some drawings

  that tell about something, such as ⌒⌒⌒ for water or ▸━D━▸ for a bow and arrow.
- Let the children use their imaginations and see if they can draw a story with pictures like the Indians did long ago. Use a paper bag cut like an animal skin to write on.
- Do a unit on Indians in America and the different types of homes they had. Why do you think they were different?

CREATIVE THINKING STARTERS:

- Do you think it would be fun to live like an Indian of long ago? What would you miss?

SUGGESTED READING:

- *North American Indians* by Marie and Douglas Gorsline. New York: Random House, 1977.
- *Little Hiawatha* by Walt Disney Productions. New York: Random House, 1978.

NOTES:

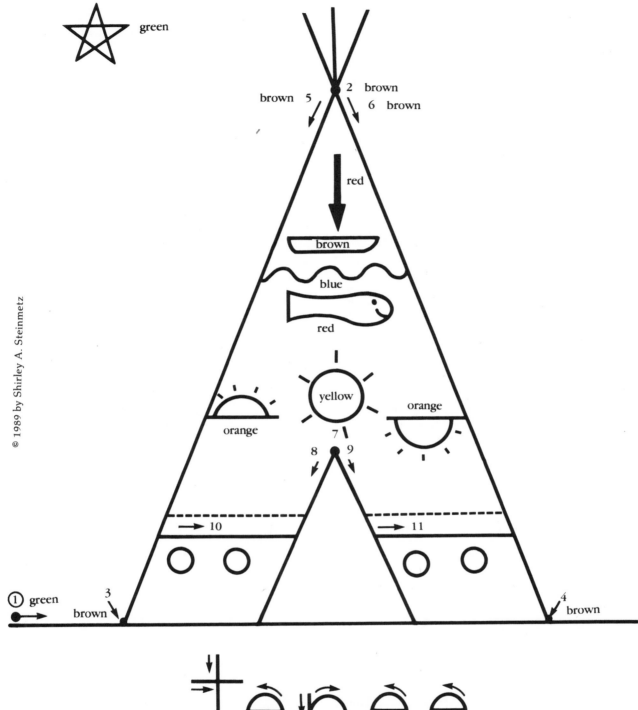

green

brown 5   2 brown
           6 brown

red

brown

blue

red

yellow

orange

orange

7
8   9

10   11

① green

3
brown

4 brown

Level I

We know our letters!

LETTER RECOGNITION
AND SOUND-LETTER CORRESPONDENCE

Here you will find seventy-eight different Silly Scribbles to help reinforce letter recognition. Each letter will have a Level I, Level II, and Level III.

SILLY SCRIBBLE TEACHER-DIRECTED PAGE

LETTER RECOGNITION: A a
SILLY SCRIBBLE: acorn
PAPER DIRECTION: "standing up"
STAR COLOR: brown

TEACHER DIRECTIONS: Look for the number 1. This will tell you where to make the START line and what color to use.

- Keep in mind the basic strokes described in Section 1.
- Always use the whole paper when doing Silly Scribbles.
- Always write the name of the Silly Scribble or encourage the children to try and write it themselves.
- Emphasize to the children that this is only one way of making an acorn. Discuss other ways.

QUESTIONS YOU COULD ASK:

- How many eyelashes did we make altogether?
- Do you know what kind of tree an acorn comes from?
- Do you know what other kinds of nuts come from trees?

ADDITIONAL ACTIVITIES:

- Go on a walking field trip near your school and pick up different kinds of nuts that have fallen to the ground. Sort them into different groups back in the classroom.
- Make an acorn tree and let each child make his or her own acorn to put on the tree. If you have enough, you can number each for a day of the month and let each child be a "squirrel" and take a nut off the tree for each day that passes. When the tree is bare, the month is over.
- Make a list of the different kinds of trees that have nuts.
- Make a collection of the different kinds of nuts we eat.

CREATIVE THINKING STARTERS:

- If you were a squirrel, how would you make acorn soup? Make a cookbook with the children's ideas.

SUGGESTED READING:

- *Miss Suzy* by Miriam Young. Illustrated by Arnold Lobel. New York: Parents Magazine Press, 1964.

NOTES:

brown

all brown

① 2 3 4 5 6 7 8 9 10 11

acorn

Level I

SILLY SCRIBBLE TEACHER-DIRECTED PAGE

Level II

LETTER RECOGNITION: A a
SILLY SCRIBBLE: nine-banded armadillo
PAPER DIRECTION: "lying down"
STAR COLOR: black

TEACHER DIRECTIONS: Look for the number 1. This will tell you where to make the START line and what color to use.

- Keep in mind the basic strokes described in Section 1.
- Always use the whole paper when doing Silly Scribbles.
- Always write the name of the Silly Scribble or encourage the children to try and write it themselves.
- Emphasize to the children that this is only one way of making an armadillo. Discuss other ways.

QUESTIONS YOU COULD ASK:

- How many zig-zag lines down did we make?
- Why do you think the armadillo has long claws?
- What sound does "armadillo" begin with?
- Did you know . . . ? By reading *The Armadillo* suggested below, you will find out that:
  — The armadillo is sometimes called "nature's little tank."
  — It has a hard, boney covering to protect it from harm.
  — Armadillos live in dens among the rocks, unplowed fields, thickets, or bushes. They burrow holes for homes.
  — The young are born in March or April, usually four at a time, either all male or all female.
  — The armadillo eats insects during the early evening or night.

ADDITIONAL ACTIVITIES:

- Pretend you are an armadillo. What would you do if a coyote came after you? A butterfly? A person?

SUGGESTED READING:

- *The Armadillo* by Theodore W. Munch and M. Vere Devault. Illustrations by Carol Rogers. Austin, Texas: Steck-Vaughn Company, 1958.
- *The Armadillo Who Had No Shell* by Sideny B. Simon. Illustrations by Walter Lorraine. New York: W. W. Norton and Company, 1966.
- *The Ten-alarm Camp-out* by Cathy Warren. Illustrated by Steven Kellogg. New York: Lothrop, Lee and Shepard, 1983.

NOTES:

© 1989 by Shirley A. Steinmetz

Level II

9 zigzag lines

all black

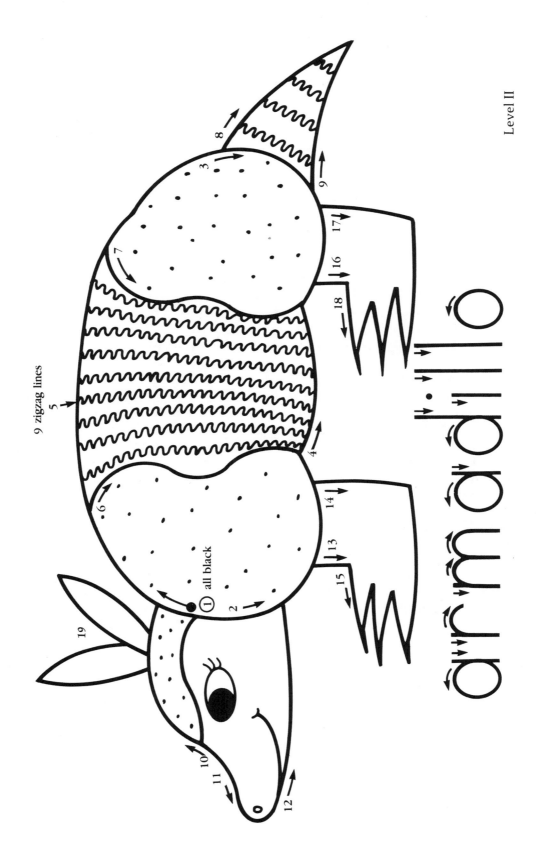

black

SILLY SCRIBBLE TEACHER-DIRECTED PAGE

Level III

LETTER RECOGNITION: A a
SILLY SCRIBBLE: anteater
PAPER DIRECTION: "standing up"
STAR COLOR: brown

TEACHER DIRECTIONS: Look for the number 1. This will tell you where to make the START line and what color to use.

- Keep in mind the basic strokes described in Section 1.
- Always use the whole paper when doing Silly Scribbles.
- Always write the name of the Silly Scribble or encourage the children to try and write it themselves.
- Emphasize to the children that this is only one way of making an anteater. Discuss other ways.

QUESTIONS YOU COULD ASK:
- What letter does "anteater" begin with?
- Why do you think it has such long claws?
- Why do you think it has such a long tongue? (one foot long)

ADDITIONAL ACTIVITIES:
- Make ten little ants. Pretend the anteater has eaten them one at a time. How many are left to zero?
- Set up an ant farm in the classroom.
- Pretend you are an anteater. What kinds of silly meals could you make using ants? (antburger, ant soup)
- Serve celery with peanut butter and raisins—you have "ants on a log"! Add peanut butter and raisins on an apple slice for "ants in a canoe"!

CREATIVE THINKING STARTERS:
- What would you do if you were an anteater who hated ants? What would you eat and what would you then be called? Draw imaginary animals to go with your new "eater". A French fry eater? An apple eater? A snake eater?

SUGGESTED READING:
- *A Is for Angry: An Animal and Adjective Alphabet* by Sandra Boynton. New York: Workman Publishing Company, 1983.

NOTES:

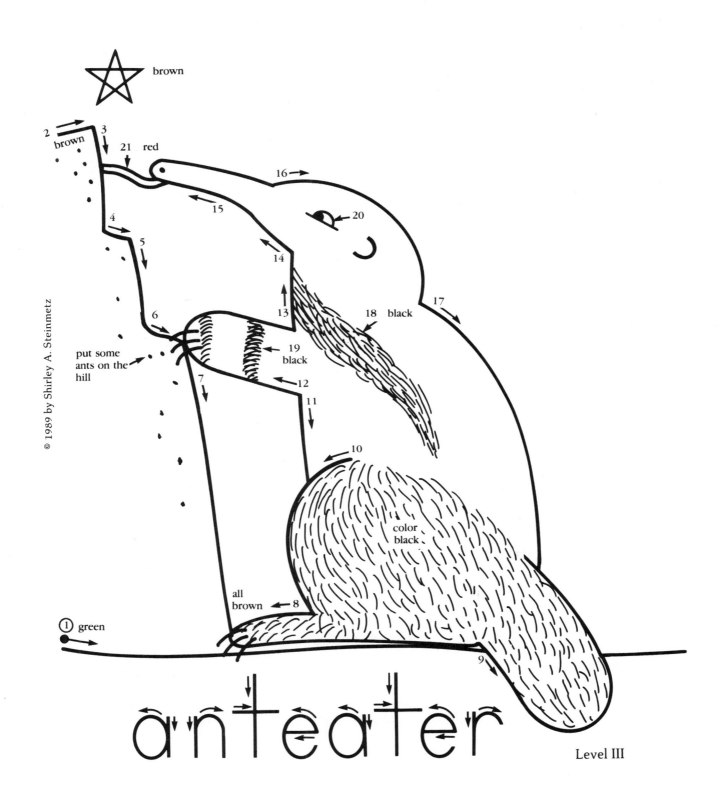

brown

2 brown 3

21 red

16

15

20

4

14

5

13

18 black

6 put some ants on the hill

19 black

17

7

12

11

10

color black

all brown ← 8

① green

9

© 1989 by Shirley A. Steinmetz

anteater

Level III

SILLY SCRIBBLE TEACHER-DIRECTED PAGE

Level I

LETTER RECOGNITION: B b
SILLY SCRIBBLE: barn
PAPER DIRECTION: "lying down"
STAR COLOR: red

TEACHER DIRECTIONS: Look for the number 1. This will tell you where to make the START line and what color to use.

- Keep in mind the basic strokes described in Section 1.
- Always use the whole paper when doing Silly Scribbles.
- Always write the name of the Silly Scribble or encourage the children to try and write it themselves.
- Emphasize to the children that this is only one way of making a barn. Discuss other ways.

QUESTIONS YOU COULD ASK:
- Which side of the barn has a fence?
- Which side of the barn has the tree?
- What kind of animals live in a barn?
- Let the children make as many animals as they want in the barnyard.
- Have a square dance and teach the children some easy dance steps. (Virginia Reel)

ADDITIONAL ACTIVITIES:
- Discuss farm animals and the different sounds they make. Play "Can You Guess What I Am?" and have different children describe or make the different sounds of farm animals to see if the others can guess what animal is being described.
- Play and sing "Old MacDonald Had a Farm."
- Make a list of farm animals and the different kinds of foods we get from them (for example, cow: milk, butter, meat, yogurt, cheese).

CREATIVE THINKING STARTERS:
- Play "What Am I?" The children act out a farm animal and the child who guesses first gets to be next.

SUGGESTED READING:
- *Early Morning in the Barn* by Nancy Tafuri. New York: Greenwillow Books, 1983.
- *Barn Dance* by Bill Martin, Jr., and John Archambault. Illustrated by Ted Rand. New York: Henry Holt and Company, 1986.

NOTES:

Level I

b ǎ r n

barn

green

brown

red

green

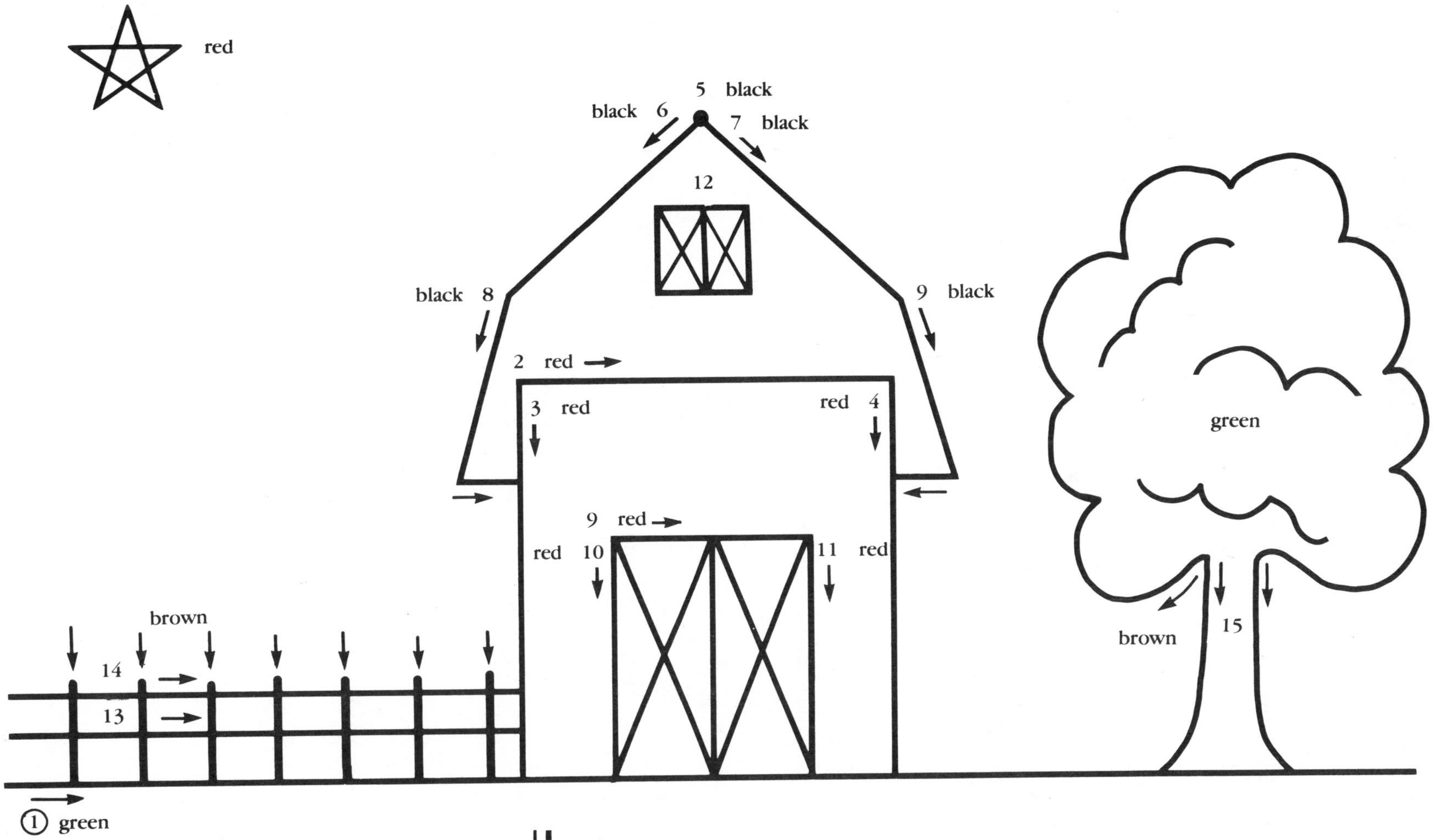

black

red

SILLY SCRIBBLE TEACHER-DIRECTED PAGE

Level II

LETTER RECOGNITION: B b
SILLY SCRIBBLE: butterfly
PAPER DIRECTION: "lying down"
STAR COLOR: purple

TEACHER DIRECTIONS: Look for the number 1. This will tell you where to make the START line and what color to use.

- Keep in mind the basic strokes described in Section 1.
- Always use the whole paper when doing Silly Scribbles.
- Always write the name of the Silly Scribble or encourage the children to try and write it themselves.
- Emphasize to the children that this is only one way of making a butterfly. Discuss other ways.

QUESTIONS YOU COULD ASK:
- How many circles did we make?
- What sound does "butterfly" begin with?
- Do you see a pattern on the butterfly? Where?

ADDITIONAL ACTIVITIES:
- Discuss how a caterpillar gets to be a butterfly.
- Have the children draw and write a sequence story about what happens.
- Invite someone in to show his or her butterfly collection.

CREATIVE THINKING STARTERS:
- Pretend you are a caterpillar and you are going to grow to be a butterfly. Can you show what happens?

SUGGESTED READING:
- *Amazing World of Butterflies and Moths* by Louis Sabin. Illustrated by Jean Helmer. Mahwah, NJ: Troll Associates, 1982.
- *The Very Hungry Caterpillar* by Eric Carle. Cleveland, OH: William Collins and World Publishing Company, 1981.

NOTES:

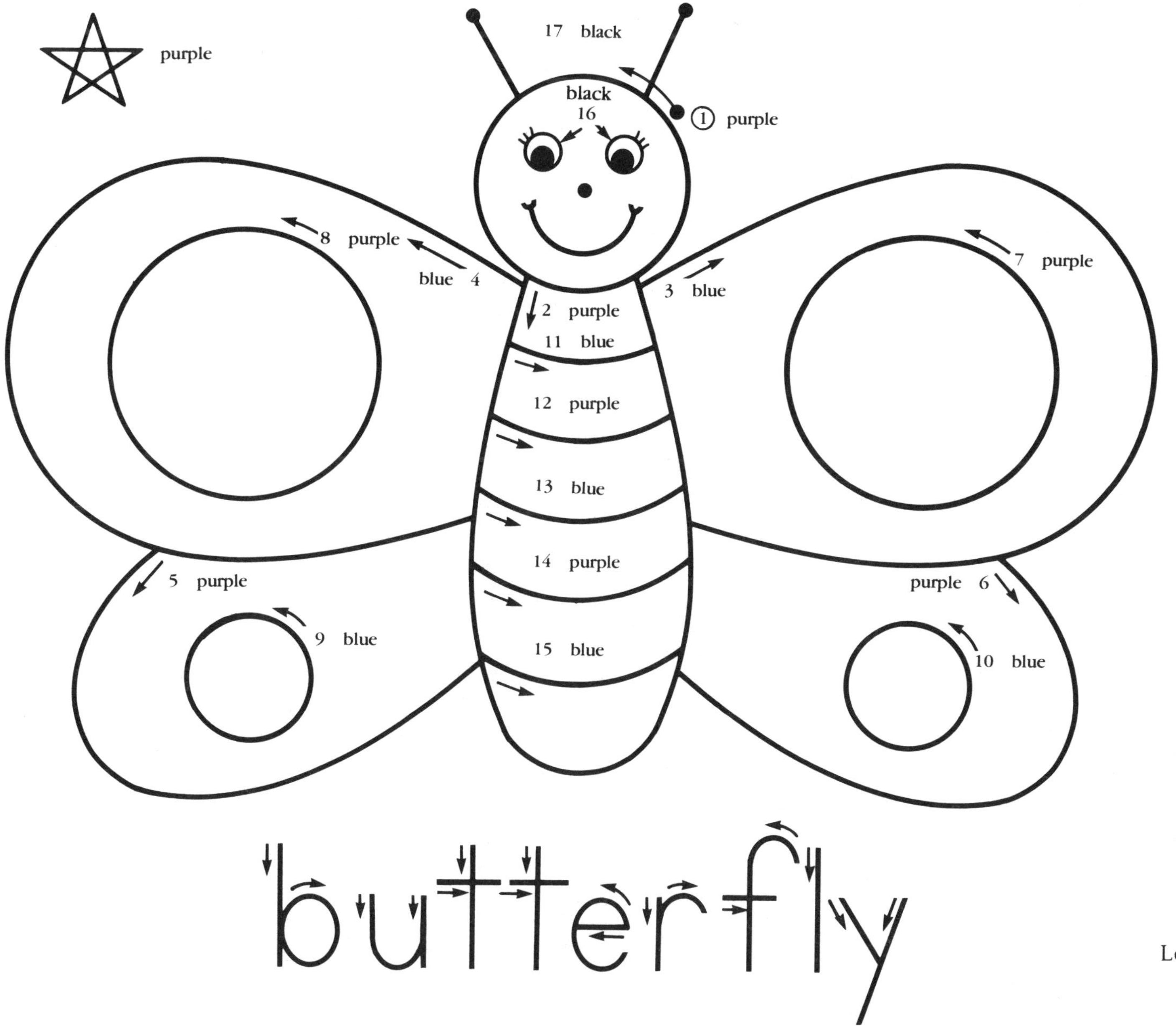
purple
17 black
black
16
① purple
8 purple
blue 4
7 purple
3 blue
2 purple
11 blue
12 purple
13 blue
14 purple
15 blue
5 purple
9 blue
purple 6
10 blue
butterfly

Level II

SILLY SCRIBBLE TEACHER-DIRECTED PAGE

Level III

LETTER RECOGNITION: B b
SILLY SCRIBBLE: badger
PAPER DIRECTION: "lying down"
STAR COLOR: black

TEACHER DIRECTIONS: Look for the number 1. This will tell you where to make the START line and what color to use.

- Keep in mind the basic strokes described in Section 1.
- Always use the whole paper when doing Silly Scribbles.
- Always write the name of the Silly Scribble or encourage the children to try and write it themselves.
- Emphasize to the children that this is only one way of making a badger. Discuss other ways.

QUESTIONS YOU COULD ASK:

- What was your first clue that it was a badger?
- What sound does "badger" begin with?
- Have you ever seen a real badger? When? Where?
- Where do you think a badger lives? What makes you think so?

ADDITIONAL ACTIVITIES:

- Have each child put his or her finger on the different part of the badger while you name the nose and tail. Next, let several of the children name parts of the badger for others to find.
- Can you make a list of the things a badger might have in its home that begin with "B"?

CREATIVE THINKING STARTERS:

- In the story *Bread and Jam for Frances* all Frances wants to eat is bread and jam. Have the children draw a picture of their favorite food; make a book of the pictures.

SUGGESTED READING:

- *Bedtime for Frances* by Russell Hoban. Illustrated by Garth Williams. New York: Harper & Row, 1960.
- *Bread and Jam for Frances* by Russell Hoban. Illustrated by Lillian Hoban. New York: Harper & Row, 1964.
- There are many other delightful stories about Frances.

NOTES:

black

© 1989 by Shirley A. Steinmetz

leave white

11

10

9

6

color in black fur

① all black

3

2

8

7

4

5

badger

Level III

SILLY SCRIBBLE TEACHER-DIRECTED PAGE

Level I

LETTER RECOGNITION: C c
SILLY SCRIBBLE: cat
PAPER DIRECTION: "standing up"
STAR COLOR: red

TEACHER DIRECTIONS: Look for the number 1. This will tell you where to make the START line and what color to use.

- Keep in mind the basic strokes described in Section 1.
- Always use the whole paper when doing Silly Scribbles.
- Always write the name of the Silly Scribble or encourage the children to try and write it themselves.
- Emphasize to the children that this is only one way of making a cat. Discuss other ways.

QUESTIONS YOU COULD ASK:

- What shape is the cat's head?
- How many whiskers did we make?
- What do you think happened to the yarn?

ADDITIONAL ACTIVITIES:

- Let the children paint different cats, and write stories about their own picture. Make a book about "If I Had a Cat."
- Play "Poor Kitty." The child chosen to be the kitten goes to another child in the circle and sits in front of him or her. Each time the kitten meows, the other child has to pet the kitten on the head while saying "Poor Kitty" without smiling. If the child smiles while saying "Poor Kitty" he or she must be the next kitten.
- Bring in a cat or visit a pet shop.

CREATIVE THINKING STARTERS:

- Find out how many different kinds of cats there are and have each child choose one to draw. Make a book of different kinds of cats doing different things.

SUGGESTED READING:

- *The Kid's Cat Book* by Tomie de Paolo. New York: Holiday House, 1960.
- *Millions of Cats* by Wanda Gag. New York: Coward-McCann, 1977.

NOTES:

red

all brown
①

8

7

black
9

2

3

4

5

6

ball of
red
yarn
10

ĉ â t

Level I

SILLY SCRIBBLE TEACHER-DIRECTED PAGE

Level II

LETTER RECOGNITION: C c
SILLY SCRIBBLE: clown
PAPER DIRECTION: "standing up"
STAR COLOR: green

TEACHER DIRECTIONS: Look for the number 1. This will tell you where to make the START line and what color to use.

- Keep in mind the basic strokes described in Section 1.
- Always use the whole paper when doing Silly Scribbles.
- Always write the name of the Silly Scribble or encourage the children to try and write it themselves.
- Emphasize to the children that this is only one way of making a clown. Discuss other ways.

QUESTIONS YOU COULD ASK:
- What was your first clue that this was a clown?
- How many buttons does the clown have?
- How many balloons does the clown have?
- Let the children fill in the clown's face.
- Have you ever seen a clown? Can you tell one thing that was silly about that clown?

ADDITIONAL ACTIVITIES:
- Have a Clown Day. Plan with the children different activities that each "clown" can do. Perhaps the children could dress as clowns, too.
- Have each child paint a picture of a clown and write or tell about it. Collect the pictures to make a book.
- Discuss the funny things clowns do that make you laugh.

CREATIVE THINKING STARTERS:
- Have a Clown Day. Let the children draw what their faces would look like. Then use face painting to try and make their faces match the pictures they drew. (Get permission from parents in case of allergies.)

SUGGESTED READING:
- *The Clown's Smile* by Mike Thaler. New York: Harper and Brothers Publishers, 1962.

NOTES:

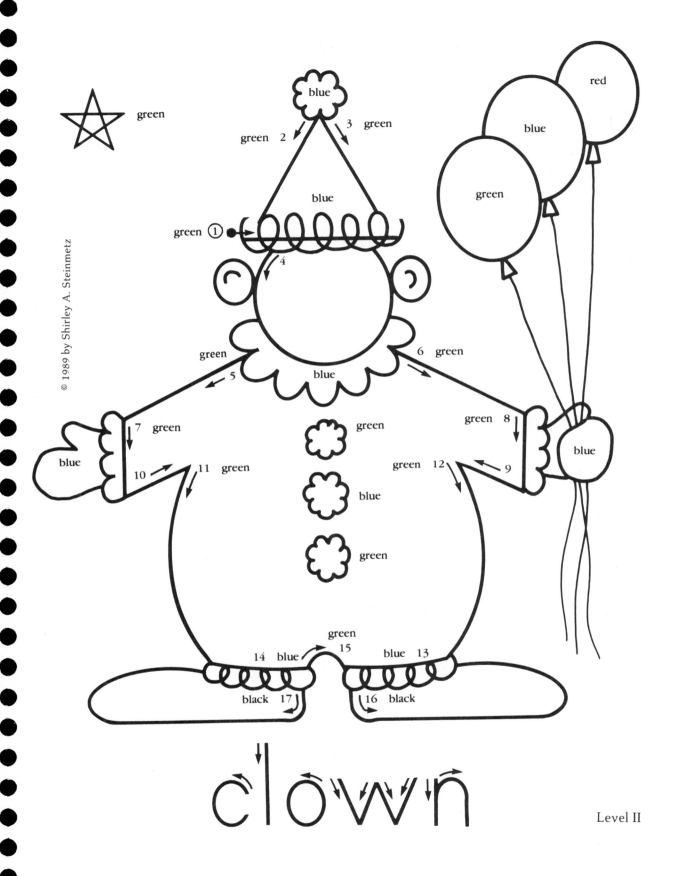

green

blue

green 2   3 green

green

blue

green ① →

4

green   6 green

5   blue

green 8

7 green   green 8

blue   blue

10   11 green   green 12   9

green

blue

green

green 15

14 blue   blue 13

black 17   16 black

© 1989 by Shirley A. Steinmetz

red

blue

green

blue

clown

Level II

SILLY SCRIBBLE TEACHER-DIRECTED PAGE

LETTER RECOGNITION: C c
SILLY SCRIBBLE: castle
PAPER DIRECTION: "lying down"
STAR COLOR: red

TEACHER DIRECTIONS: Look for the number 1. This will tell you where to make the START line and what color to use.

- Keep in mind the basic strokes described in Section 1.
- Always use the whole paper when doing Silly Scribbles.
- Always write the name of the Silly Scribble or encourage the children to try and write it themselves.
- Emphasize to the children that this is only one way of making a castle. Discuss other ways.

QUESTIONS YOU COULD ASK:
- Which line did you make first?
- What shape are the windows?
- How many ovals are there?
- Let the children finish the picture by drawing who they think lives in this castle. Share the pictures.

ADDITIONAL ACTIVITIES:
- Set up a sandbox area in your room. Provide moist sand and small containers with which to mold sand and encourage the children to make their own castles.
- Encourage the children to make castles out of different media, such as cut-out paper or fabric, wooden blocks, or Styrofoam.
- Make a book about "If I Lived in a Castle." Have each child draw what his or her castle would look like and write or tell about it.

CREATIVE THINKING STARTERS:
- Does a dragon live near your castle? If so, what does it look like? How does it act? Draw and write about it.

SUGGESTED READING:
- There are many stories with castles, such as *Sleeping Beauty* by the Brothers Grimm. Ask your school librarian.

NOTES:

© 1989 by Shirley A. Steinmetz

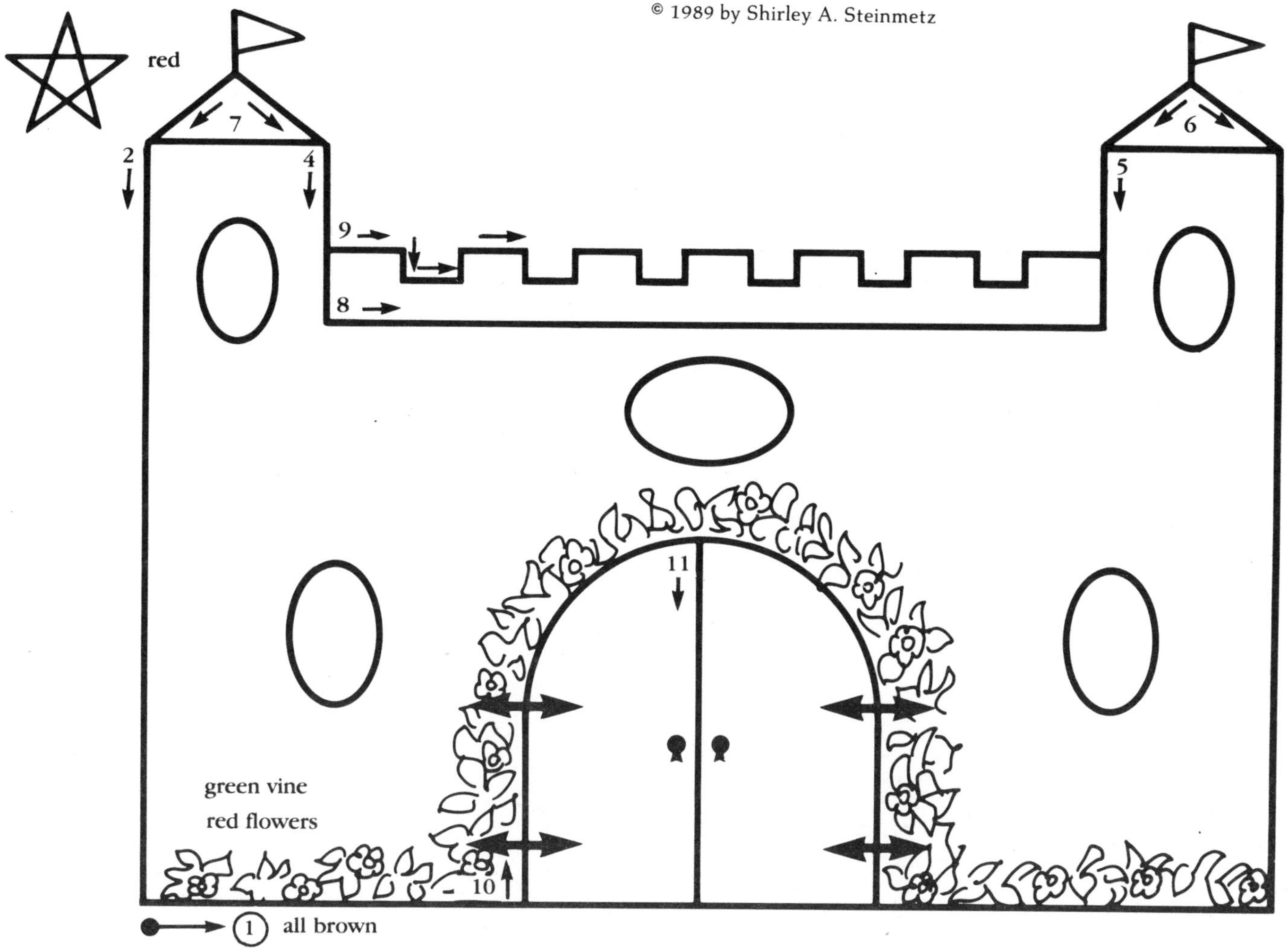

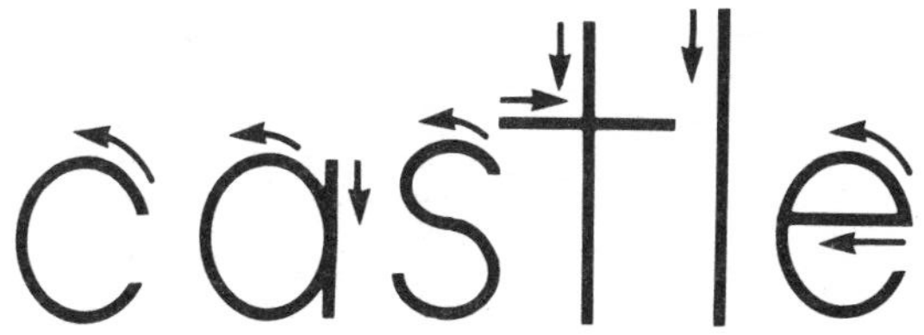

green vine
red flowers

① all brown

red

cåstle

Level III

SILLY SCRIBBLE TEACHER-DIRECTED PAGE

Level I

LETTER RECOGNITION: D d
SILLY SCRIBBLE: dog and doghouse
PAPER DIRECTION: "lying down"
STAR COLOR: red

TEACHER DIRECTIONS: Look for the number 1. This will tell you where to make the START line and what color to use.

- Keep in mind the basic strokes described in Section 1.
- Always use the whole paper when doing Silly Scribbles.
- Always write the name of the Silly Scribble or encourage the children to try and write it themselves.
- Emphasize to the children that this is only one way of making a doghouse. Discuss other ways.

QUESTIONS YOU COULD ASK:
- Whose house is this?
- Can you make a dog that you think would live in this house?
- What kind of dog did you make?

ADDITIONAL ACTIVITIES:
- Discuss pets. Let the children draw and write about their pets.
- Make ten doghouses with a number from 1 to 10 on each house. Have the children make a dog to live in each house. Using small sticky circles, put dots on each dog using amounts from one to ten. See if the children can match the dog to the correct house.
- Play "Doggie, Doggie, Who Has Your Bone?" Make a little paper bone. Have a child be the "dog" and sit on a chair with his or her back to the other children. Place the dog bone behind the chair. One child sneaks up to get the bone, then hides it behind his or her back. Then all children say "Doggie, Doggie, who has your bone?" The "dog" turns around and gets three guesses. If he or she does not guess who has the bone, the child who does have it gets to be the new "dog."

SUGGESTED READING:
- *Doghouse for Sale* by Donna Lugg Pape. Illustrated by Tom Eaton. Champaign, IL: Garrard Publishing, 1979.

NOTES:

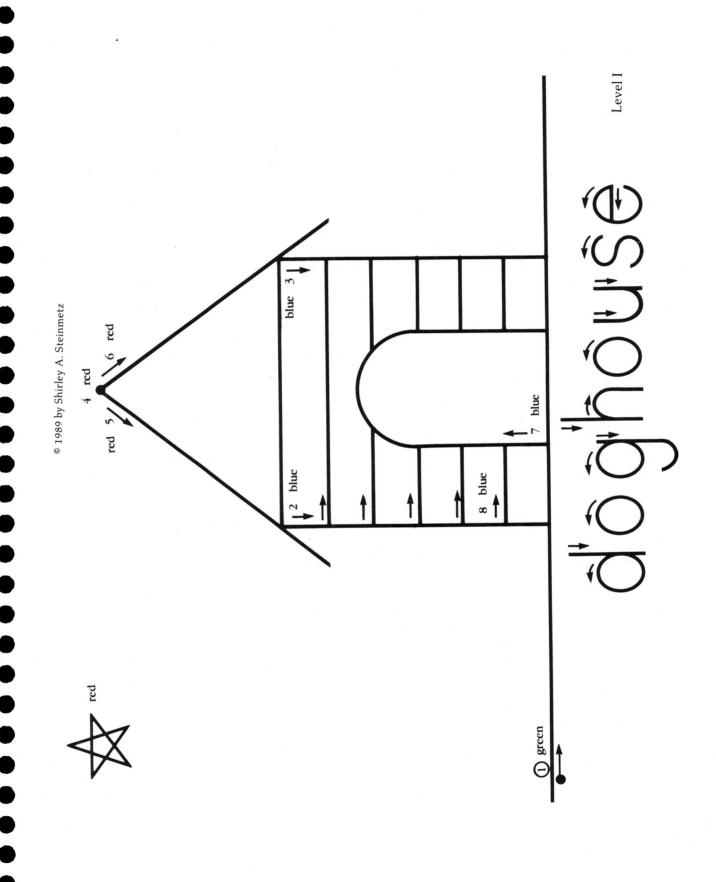

doghouse

Level I

© 1989 by Shirley A. Steinmetz

SILLY SCRIBBLE TEACHER-DIRECTED PAGE

Level II

LETTER RECOGNITION: D d
SILLY SCRIBBLE: doll
PAPER DIRECTION: "standing up"
STAR COLOR: blue

TEACHER DIRECTIONS: Look for the number 1. This will tell you where to make the START line and what color to use.

- Keep in mind the basic strokes described in Section 1.
- Always use the whole paper when doing Silly Scribbles.
- Always write the name of the Silly Scribble or encourage the children to try and write it themselves.
- Emphasize to the children that this is only one way of making a doll. Discuss other ways.

QUESTIONS YOU COULD ASK:
- What is the pattern on the doll's socks?
- What shape is the doll's head?
- Finish the doll's face the way you want it to look.
- Which line did you make first? Last?

ADDITIONAL ACTIVITIES:
- Have a discussion about rag dolls. Discuss how floppy they are. (If you have one, let the children hold and play with it.) Have the children pretend to be a rag doll and discuss how the arms, legs, and head would be if they were floppy,. Can you stand up? Fall down? Stand up, then bend over?
- Have a Doll Day and let the children bring in their favorite dolls or stuffed toys. Share these.

CREATIVE THINKING STARTERS:
- If you were a doll, whom would you like to belong to? Why?

SUGGESTED READING:
- There are many Raggedy Ann and Andy stories written by Johnny Gruelle to choose from. Ask your librarian for suggestions.
- *Mommy, Buy Me a China Doll* adapted from an Ozark children's song by Harve Zemach. Illustrated by Margot Zemach. New York: Farrar, Straus, and Giroux, 1966.
- *The Lonely Doll* by Dare Wright. New York: Doubleday & Company, 1957.

NOTES:

blue

blue

blue

red curls

red 3

red 4

red 5

2 red

6 red

blue → 13

14

blue

red 7

9 red

10

11

red 8

blue 12 →

15 blue

blue 16

17 blue

18

blue with red lines

19

21 black

20 black

dŏll

Level II

SILLY SCRIBBLE TEACHER-DIRECTED PAGE

LETTER RECOGNITION: D d
SILLY SCRIBBLE: dinosaur
PAPER DIRECTION: "lying down"
STAR COLOR: brown

TEACHER DIRECTIONS: Look for the number 1. This will tell you where to make the START line and what color to use.

- Keep in mind the basic strokes described in Section 1.
- Always use the whole paper when doing Silly Scribbles.
- Always write the name of the Silly Scribble or encourage the children to try and write it themselves.
- Emphasize to the children that this is only one way of making a dinosaur. Discuss other ways.

QUESTIONS YOU COULD ASK:

- Do you know what kind of dinosaur this is? (stegosaurus)
- How many bony plates did we make on its back?
- Do you think this dinosaur ate leaves or meat?
- How can you tell? What makes you think so?
- Which line did you make first?

ADDITIONAL ACTIVITIES:

- Pretend you are a dinosaur. Show me how you would move.
- Bring in lots of reference pictures, books, models, and so forth. Make a list of all of the dinosaurs that the children know.
- Have the children draw, paint, or cut and paste their favorite dinosaur. Have the children tell or write about their pictures. Make a book of them.

CREATIVE THINKING STARTERS:

- What would you do if you found a dinosaur egg and right before your eyes it hatched?

SUGGESTED READING:

- *The Secret Dinosaur* by Marilyn Hirsh. New York: Holiday House, 1979.
- *Isadore the Dinosaur* by Tom LaFleur and Gale Brennan. Illustrated by Meri Howlett Berghauer. Milwaukee: Ideals Publishing Corp., 1981.

NOTES:

© 1989 by Shirley A. Steinmetz

Level III

brown

all brown

dinosaur

SILLY SCRIBBLE TEACHER-DIRECTED PAGE

Level I

LETTER RECOGNITION: E e
SILLY SCRIBBLE: egg
PAPER DIRECTION: "standing up"
STAR COLOR: brown

TEACHER DIRECTIONS: Look for the number 1. This will tell you where to make the START line and what color to use.

- Keep in mind the basic strokes described in Section 1.
- Always use the whole paper when doing Silly Scribbles.
- Always write the name of the Silly Scribble or encourage the children to try and write it themselves.
- Emphasize to the children that this is only one way of making an egg. Discuss other ways.

QUESTIONS YOU COULD ASK:
- What sound does "egg" begin with?
- What is happening to the egg?
- What is in the egg?

ADDITIONAL ACTIVITIES:
- Have the children turn the Silly Scribble over and draw what they think is in the egg. Share their stories.
- Color the eggs, even if it isn't Easter!
- Have the children help you make eight different-colored egg yolks and whites to look like a "sunny-side-up" egg. Make matching pans for each egg with the color word written on each pan. Can the children "cook" the correct egg in the matching pan?
- Have a "spoon and egg" race. Be careful not to drop them!
- Have an egg roll by pushing an egg with your nose.

SUGGESTED READING:
- *Horton Hatches the Egg* by Dr. Seuss. New York: Random House, 1940.
- *Green Eggs and Ham* by Dr. Seuss. New York: Random House, 1960.

NOTES:

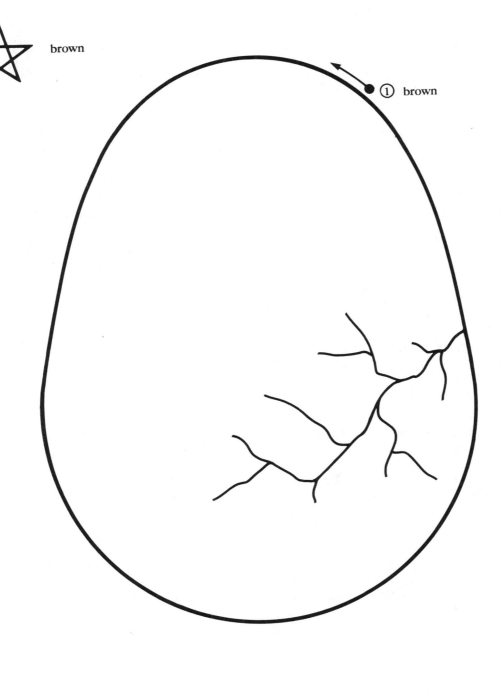

brown

① brown

e g g

Level I

SILLY SCRIBBLE TEACHER-DIRECTED PAGE

Level II

LETTER RECOGNITION: E e
SILLY SCRIBBLE: elf
PAPER DIRECTION: "standing up"
STAR COLOR: green

TEACHER DIRECTIONS: Look for the number 1. This will tell you where to make the START line and what color to use.

- Keep in mind the basic strokes described in Section 1.
- Always use the whole paper when doing Silly Scribbles.
- Always write the name of the Silly Scribble or encourage the children to try and write it themselves.
- Emphasize to the children that this is only one way of making an elf. Discuss other ways.

QUESTIONS YOU COULD ASK:

- Do you know what size an elf is?
- Why do you think the elf is dressed in green?
- Do you think there is such a thing as an elf?
- What sound does "elf" begin with?

ADDITIONAL ACTIVITIES:

- Draw, paint, or cut and paste a picture of an elf. Tell or write about it.
- What do you think a "rainbow" elf would look like? A "star" elf?
- Discuss leprechauns. What would you wish for if you caught one?

CREATIVE THINKING STARTERS:

- If you had an elf of your very own, what would it do? Design a little house for the elf to live in by using a box.

SUGGESTED READING:

- *The Blueberry Pie Elf* by Jane Thayer. Illustrated by Seymour Fleishman. New York: William Morrow and Co., 1961.
- *Long Ago Elf* by Mary and R. A. Smith. New York: Follett Publishing Co., 1968.
- *The Elves and the Shoemaker* by the Brothers Grimm. There are many different copies of this story, so ask your librarian for one.

NOTES:

green

4 green

green 2

3 green

① brown

red hair

5

red 6

7 green

8 green

9 green

green 10

green 14 11

12 13 green

15 green

16 green

green 17

18 19

23 20

22 21

green green

elf

Level II

SILLY SCRIBBLE TEACHER-DIRECTED PAGE

Level III

LETTER RECOGNITION: E e
SILLY SCRIBBLE: elephant
PAPER DIRECTION: "lying down"
STAR COLOR: black

TEACHER DIRECTIONS: Look for the number 1. This will tell you where to make the START line and what color to use.

- Keep in mind the basic strokes described in Section 1.
- Always use the whole paper when doing Silly Scribbles.
- Always write the name of the Silly Scribble or encourage the children to try and write it themselves.
- Emphasize to the children that this is only one way of making an elephant. Discuss other ways.

QUESTIONS YOU COULD ASK:
- What sound does "elephant" begin with?
- Is there any animal bigger than an elephant?
- What is the nose of an elephant called?
- What do you think the elephant uses its tusks for?

ADDITIONAL ACTIVITIES:
- Watch a video or movie about elephants or look at elephant photos. Discuss the difference between Asian and African elephants.
- Pretend you're an elephant. How would you walk?
- Play "Pin the Tail on the Elephant."
- Share elephant jokes.

CREATIVE THINKING STARTERS:
- Do you know why an elephant has baggy knees?

SUGGESTED READING:
- *Elephant* by Byron Barton. New York: Seabury Press, 1971.
- Enjoy any *Babar* story by Laurent de Brunhoff.

NOTES:

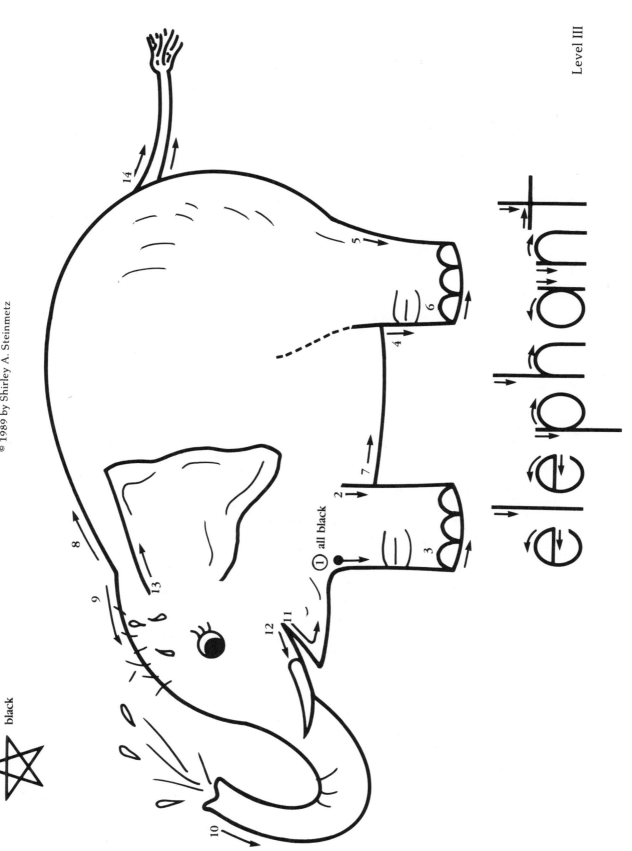

© 1989 by Shirley A. Steinmetz

black

Level III

elephant

SILLY SCRIBBLE TEACHER-DIRECTED PAGE

Level I

LETTER RECOGNITION: F f
SILLY SCRIBBLE: frog
PAPER DIRECTION: "lying down"
STAR COLOR: green

TEACHER DIRECTIONS: Look for the number 1. This will tell you where to make the START line and what color to use.

- Keep in mind the basic strokes described in Section 1.
- Always use the whole paper when doing Silly Scribbles.
- Always write the name of the Silly Scribble or encourage the children to try and write it themselves.
- Emphasize to the children that this is only one way of making a frog. Discuss other ways.

QUESTIONS YOU COULD ASK:
- What sound does "frog" begin with?
- Why do you think the frog is smiling? Do you think real frogs smile?
- Do you know what a frog says?
- Which line did you make first? Last?

ADDITIONAL ACTIVITIES:
- Play "leap frog."
- Make ten lily pads and number them from 1 to 10. Lay them on the floor and let a child be the frog. Can he or she hop the lily pads in order?
- Bring in a real frog and set up a home for it in an old aquarium. Observe the frog and discuss.
- Watch a video or movie or show photos about frogs and toads. Compare and discuss the difference between frogs and toads.

SUGGESTED READING:
- *Jump, Frog, Jump* by Robert Kalan. Illustrated by Byron Barton. New York: Greenwillow Books, 1981.
- *Frog and Toad Together* by Arnold Lobel. New York: Harper & Row, 1971, 1972.
- *Why Frogs Are Wet* by Judy Hawes. Illustrated by Don Madden. Toronto: Fitzhenry and Whiteside Limited, 1968.

NOTES:

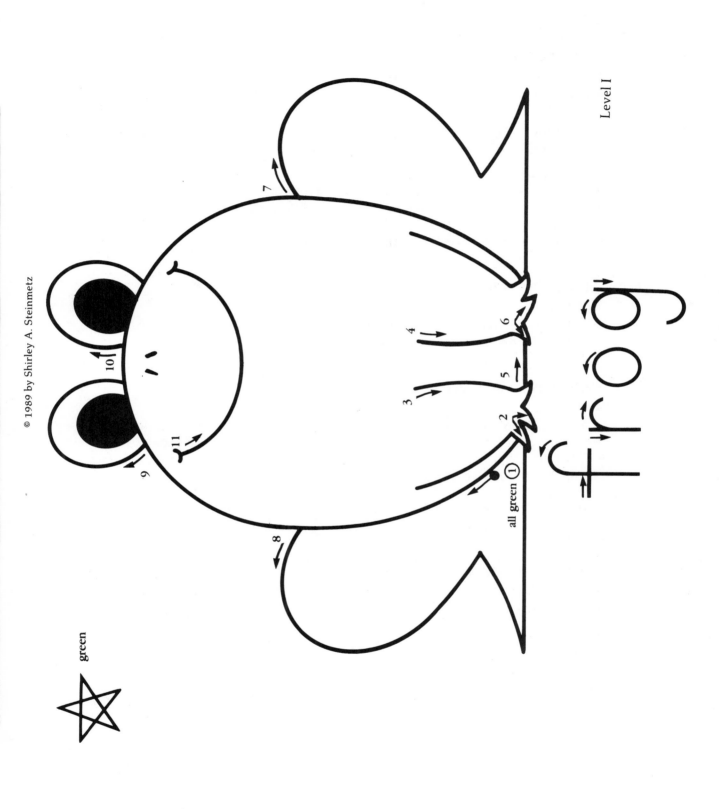

© 1989 by Shirley A. Steinmetz

all green ①

frog

green

Level I

SILLY SCRIBBLE TEACHER-DIRECTED PAGE

Level II

LETTER RECOGNITION: F f
SILLY SCRIBBLE: flamingo
PAPER DIRECTION: "standing up"
STAR COLOR: red

TEACHER DIRECTIONS: Look for the number 1. This will tell you where to make the START line and what color to use.

- Keep in mind the basic strokes described in Section 1.
- Always use the whole paper when doing Silly Scribbles.
- Always write the name of the Silly Scribble or encourage the children to try and write it themselves.
- Emphasize to the children that this is only one way of making a flamingo. Discuss other ways.

QUESTIONS YOU COULD ASK:
- What was your first clue that it was a flamingo?
- What sound(s) does "flamingo" begin with?
- Where is the flamingo standing?
- Where is the other leg?

ADDITIONAL ACTIVITIES:
- Pretend you are a flamingo. Can you stand on one leg?
- Discuss "ing" used in words. Make a list of "ing" words.
- Let the children use pink paint and make a flamingo on blue paper.
- Write a collaborative story about a flamingo that hated the warm weather and wanted to live at the North Pole.

CREATIVE THINKING STARTERS:
- Why do you think the flamingo has such long legs? What might the flamingo do differently if it had short legs?

SUGGESTED READING:
- *Have You Seen Birds?* by Joanne Oppenheim. Illustrated by Barbara Reid. Ontario: Scholastic-TAB Publications Ltd., 1986 (original text 1968).

NOTES:

red

all light red

① 2

11

yellow with black

4

color black

3

5

6

9

8

7

10

12 blue smile lines

flamingo

Level II

SILLY SCRIBBLE TEACHER-DIRECTED PAGE

Level III

LETTER RECOGNITION: F f
SILLY SCRIBBLE: fox
PAPER DIRECTION: "standing up"
STAR COLOR: red

TEACHER DIRECTIONS: Look for the number 1. This will tell you where to make the START line and what color to use.

- Keep in mind the basic strokes described in Section 1.
- Always use the whole paper when doing Silly Scribbles.
- Always write the name of the Silly Scribble or encourage the children to try and write it themselves.
- Emphasize to the children that this is only one way of making a fox. Discuss other ways.

QUESTIONS YOU COULD ASK:

- Why do you only see one eye on our fox?
- What letter does "fox" begin with?
- Can you think of any numbers that begin with "f"?
- Which line did you make first?

ADDITIONAL ACTIVITIES:

- If it is snowing outside, you can play "Fox and Geese."
- Make a list of the words that rhyme with "fox."

CREATIVE THINKING STARTERS:

- Tell the story of *The Gingerbread Boy* After discussing the sequence, let the children act it out. Encourage the children to make up alternative endings to the story.

SUGGESTED READING:

- *Fox in Socks* by Dr. Seuss. New York: Random House, 1956.
- *Fox Eyes* by Margaret Wise Brown. Illustrations by Garth Williams. New York: Pantheon, 1951.
- *Little Fox Goes to the End of the World* by Ann Tompert. Illustrated by John Wallner. New York: Crown Publishers, 1976.

NOTES:

red

14

4

3

16

15

2 ① all brown (when coloring use brown and red)

5

6

7

8

12

13

9

11

10

© 1989 by Shirley A. Steinmetz

fox

Level III

SILLY SCRIBBLE TEACHER-DIRECTED PAGE

LETTER RECOGNITION: G g
SILLY SCRIBBLE: groundhog
PAPER DIRECTION: "standing up"
STAR COLOR: brown

TEACHER DIRECTIONS: Look for the number 1. This will tell you where to make the START line and what color to use.

- Keep in mind the basic strokes described in Section 1.
- Always use the whole paper when doing Silly Scribbles.
- Always write the name of the Silly Scribble or encourage the children to try and write it themselves.
- Emphasize to the children that this is only one way of making a groundhog. Discuss other ways.

QUESTIONS YOU COULD ASK:
- What letter does "groundhog" begin with?
- Where is the rest of the groundhog?
- Is the groundhog coming or going?
- How many circles did we make?

ADDITIONAL ACTIVITIES:
- Call your local weather station and find out the name of the groundhog that your area watches on Groundhog Day. Encourage the children to watch the news to see what happens.
- Let the children predict what will happen on Groundhog Day. Keep a chart.

CREATIVE THINKING STARTERS:
- Make a sequence book about what happens on Groundhog Day. Have the children draw the pictures and write what happens. Your book should have two endings.

SUGGESTED READING:
- *Waldo the Woodchuck* by Tony Palazzo. New York: Duell, Sloan and Pearce, 1964.
- *The Little Lost Shadow* by Edith W. Boutelle. Illustrations by Robert Pierce. Middletown, CT: Weekly Reader Books, Xerox Corporation, 1981.

NOTES:

 brown

groundhog

Level I

SILLY SCRIBBLE TEACHER-DIRECTED PAGE

Level II

LETTER RECOGNITION: G g
SILLY SCRIBBLE: gorilla
PAPER DIRECTION: "standing up"
STAR COLOR: brown

TEACHER DIRECTIONS: Look for the number 1. This will tell you where to make the START line and what color to use.

- Keep in mind the basic strokes described in Section 1.
- Always use the whole paper when doing Silly Scribbles.
- Always write the name of the Silly Scribble or encourage the children to try and write it themselves.
- Emphasize to the children that this is only one way of making a gorilla. Discuss other ways.

QUESTIONS YOU COULD ASK:

- What was your first clue that it was a gorilla?
- What letter does "gorilla" begin with?
- How many circles did we make?
- Where is the rest of the gorilla? Why isn't it on the paper?

ADDITIONAL ACTIVITIES:

- Make gifts for the gorilla that begin with "G." (Thanks, Susan Klotz.)
- Let the children paint a gorilla at the easel.
- Watch a video or movie or look at pictures of gorillas. Discuss and list all the things the class knows about gorillas.
- Go to a zoo to observe a gorilla.
- Rent a gorilla suit. Put it on while the children watch you (so you don't frighten anyone) and discuss each piece of the costume. Pretend you are a gorilla. Let the children take turns wearing the mask. Discuss wearing costumes.

CREATIVE THINKING STARTERS:

- Why do you think this gorilla is grinning?

SUGGESTED READING:

- *Great Gorilla Grins* by Beth Hilgartner. Illustrations by Leslie Morrill. Boston: Little, Brown and Co., 1979.
- *Julius* by Syd Hoff. New York: Harper and Brothers, 1959.
- *Gorilla* by Anthony Browne. New York: Alfred A. Knopf, 1983.

NOTES:

brown

① all brown

(yellow inside)

© 1989 by Shirley A. Steinmetz

gorilla

Level II

SILLY SCRIBBLE TEACHER-DIRECTED PAGE

Level III

LETTER RECOGNITION: G g
SILLY SCRIBBLE: goose
PAPER DIRECTION: "lying down"
STAR COLOR: blue

TEACHER DIRECTIONS: Look for the number 1. This will tell you where to make the START line and what color to use.

- Keep in mind the basic strokes described in Section 1.
- Always use the whole paper when doing Silly Scribbles.
- Always write the name of the Silly Scribble or encourage the children to try and write it themselves.
- Emphasize to the children that this is only one way of making a goose. Discuss other ways.

QUESTIONS YOU COULD ASK:
- What sound does "goose" begin with?
- What is the father called? The mother? The baby?
- Where are they going?
- Which line did you make first to make a goose?

ADDITIONAL ACTIVITIES:
- Play "Match the Families." Have pictures of animal families and let the children match the parent with the child. This could then be used as a concentration or memory game.
- Can you think of any words that rhyme with "goose"?
- Read the story *The Golden Goose* by the Brothers Grimm. Discuss the sequence and let the children retell the story.

CREATIVE THINKING STARTERS:
- Make a list of animals and what the babies are called (such as cub, pup, chick). Make a book of the names.

SUGGESTED READING:
- *Silly Goose* by Jack Kent. Englewood Cliffs, NJ: Prentice Hall, 1983.
- Enjoy any of the *Petunia* stories by Roger Duvoisin, published by Knopf.

NOTES:

blue

© 1989 by Shirley A. Steinmetz

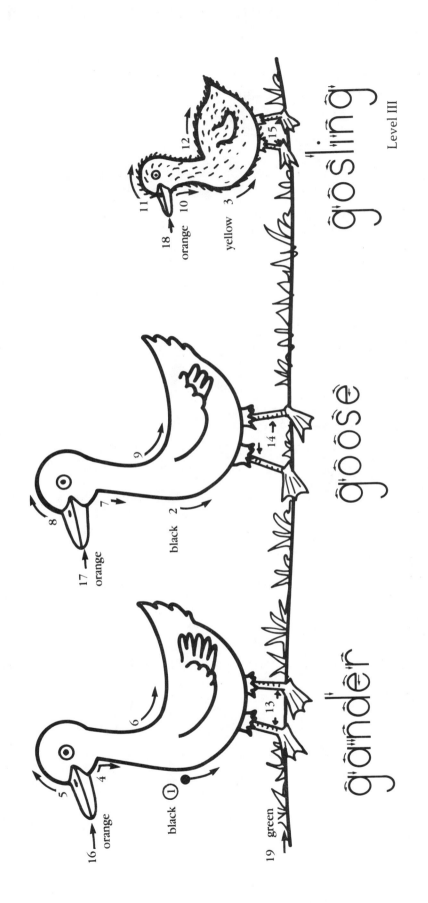

gander

goose

gosling

Level III

SILLY SCRIBBLE TEACHER-DIRECTED PAGE

LETTER RECOGNITION: H h
SILLY SCRIBBLE: hiding
PAPER DIRECTION: "lying down"
STAR COLOR: blue

TEACHER DIRECTIONS: Look for the number 1. This will tell you where to make the START line and what color to use.

- Keep in mind the basic strokes described in Section 1.
- Always use the whole paper when doing Silly Scribbles.
- Always write the name of the Silly Scribble or encourage the children to try and write it themselves.
- Emphasize to the children that this is only one way of making a "hiding" picture. Discuss other ways.

QUESTIONS YOU COULD ASK:

- What sound does "hiding" begin with?
- What is hiding?
- What kind of day is it?

ADDITIONAL ACTIVITIES:

- Play "Hide and Seek."
- Play "Where Is Stan?" Make a small Stan out of posterboard. Hide him somewhere in the room while the children cover their eyes. Hide him where he can still be seen. The child who can tell you where Stan is and use correct spatial relationship words gets to hide Stan next. Encourage the children to use a sentence.
- Look at photos of animals that "hide" by using camouflage. Why do you think they need to hide?
- Let the children make their own "hiding" pictures and share them.

CREATIVE THINKING STARTERS:

- Why do you see only part of the animal? Where is the rest? How would you know where the animal was hiding if you didn't see a little bit to give you a clue?

SUGGESTED READING:

- *Where Can an Elephant Hide?* by David McPhail. New York: Doubleday, 1979.
- *My Secret Hiding Place* by Rose Greydanus. Illustrated by Paul Harvey. Mahwah, NJ: Troll Associates, 1980.

NOTES:

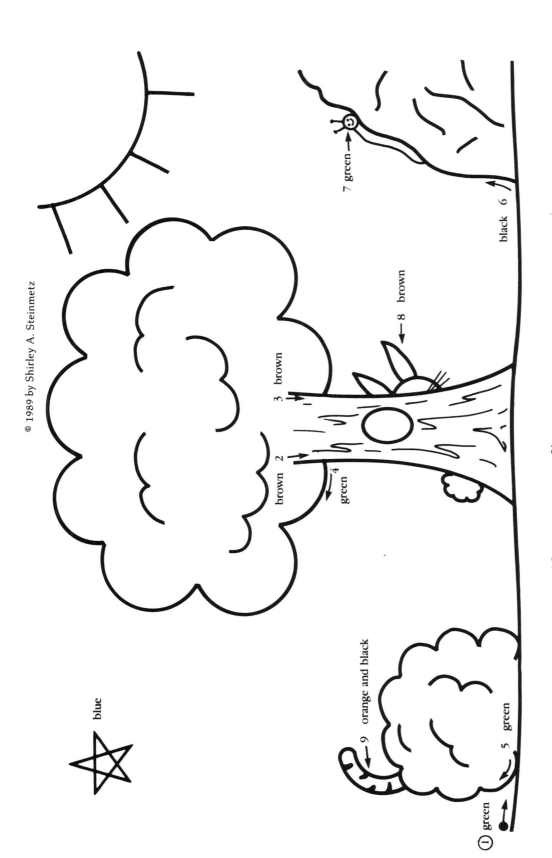

© 1989 by Shirley A. Steinmetz

blue

9 orange and black

5 green

1 green

brown 2

green 4

3 brown

8 brown

black 6

7 green

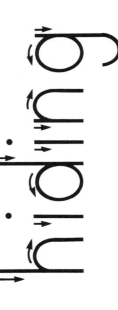

hiding

SILLY SCRIBBLE TEACHER-DIRECTED PAGE

Level II

LETTER RECOGNITION: H h
SILLY SCRIBBLE: hedgehog
PAPER DIRECTION: "lying down"
STAR COLOR: brown

TEACHER DIRECTIONS: Look for the number 1. This will tell you where to make the START line and what color to use.

- Keep in mind the basic strokes described in Section 1.
- Always use the whole paper when doing Silly Scribbles.
- Always write the name of the Silly Scribble or encourage the children to try and write it themselves.
- Emphasize to the children that this is only one way of making a hedgehog. Discuss other ways.

QUESTIONS YOU COULD ASK:
- What sound does "hedgehog" end with?
- Have you ever seen a hedgehog?
- Did you know that hedgehogs roll into a ball when threatened?

ADDITIONAL ACTIVITIES:
- Can you curl up into a ball like a hedgehog?
- Can you think of some other names for a hedgehog?
- Write a list of words that rhyme with "hog."

CREATIVE THINKING STARTERS:
- Since the hedgehog can be tamed and kept as a pet, what reasons would you give to have one for your very own? What do you think your parents would say?
- Why do you think the hedgehog has "hog" in its name? Can you find out why?

SUGGESTED READING:
- *Prickly Pig* by Gillian McClure. London: André Deutsch Limited, 1979. Limited, 1979.

NOTES:

brown

all brown ①

hedgehog

SILLY SCRIBBLE TEACHER-DIRECTED PAGE

Level III

LETTER RECOGNITION: H h
SILLY SCRIBBLE: hippopotamus
PAPER DIRECTION: "lying down"
STAR COLOR: black

TEACHER DIRECTIONS: Look for the number 1. This will tell you where to make the START line and what color to use.

- Keep in mind the basic strokes described in Section 1.
- Always use the whole paper when doing Silly Scribbles.
- Always write the name of the Silly Scribble or encourage the children to try and write it themselves.
- Emphasize to the children that this is only one way of making a hippopotamus. Discuss other ways.

QUESTIONS YOU COULD ASK:
- What was your first clue that it was a hippopotamus?
- How many letters are in the word "hippopotamus"?
- Do you know what a hippopotamus eats? (125 or more pounds of grass, vegetables, and fruits *each day*)

ADDITIONAL ACTIVITIES:
- Discuss and make a list of all the things we know about the hippopotamus.
- The hungry hippo needs "H" things to eat. Can you think of any?

CREATIVE THINKING STARTERS:
- How would you like a hippopotamus for a pet? What would you need if you did have a pet hippo?

SUGGESTED READING:
- *Lonely Veronica* by Roger Duvoisin. New York: Alfred A. Knopf, 1963.
- *Hot Hippo* by Mwenye Hadithi. Illustrated by Adrienne Kennaway. Boston: Little, Brown and Company, 1986.
- *There's a Hippopotamus Under My Bed* by Mike Thaler. Illustrated by Ray Cruz. New York: Franklin Watts, 1977.

NOTES:

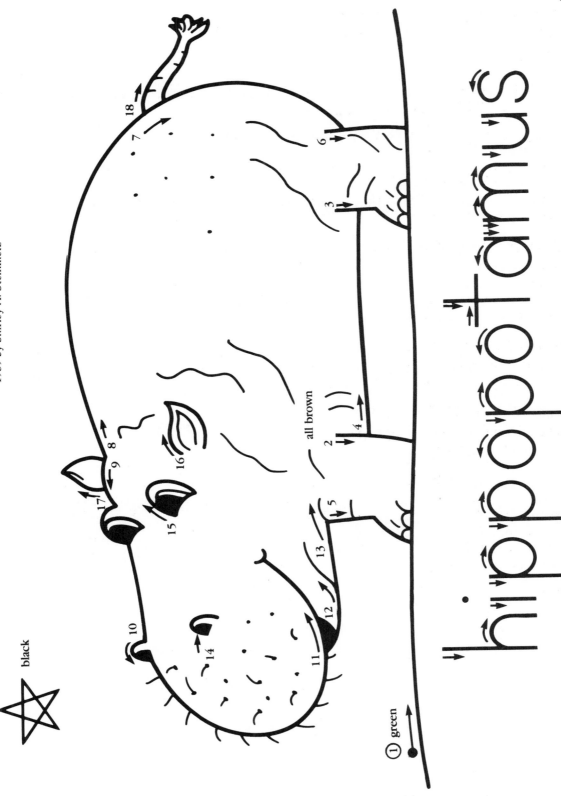

© 1989 by Shirley A. Steinmetz

black

all brown

① green

hippopotamus

Level III

SILLY SCRIBBLE TEACHER-DIRECTED PAGE

LETTER RECOGNITION: I i
SILLY SCRIBBLE: igloo
PAPER DIRECTION: "lying down"
STAR COLOR: black

TEACHER DIRECTIONS: Look for the number 1. This will tell you where to make the START line and what color to use.

- Keep in mind the basic strokes described in Section 1.
- Always use the whole paper when doing Silly Scribbles.
- Always write the name of the Silly Scribble or encourage the children to try and write it themselves.
- Emphasize to the children that this is only one way of making an igloo. Discuss other ways.

QUESTIONS YOU COULD ASK:

- What sound does "igloo" begin with?
- Who lives in an igloo?
- What is an igloo made out of?
- Which line did you make first?

ADDITIONAL ACTIVITIES:

- Cut and paste your own igloo out of white paper.
- Discuss why Eskimos made their homes out of ice. Why not wood?
- Discuss what it might be like to live in an igloo.

CREATIVE THINKING STARTERS:

- If you lived in an igloo, what would the inside look like?

SUGGESTED READING:

- *The Penguin That Hated the Cold*, adapted by Barbara Brenner from Walt Disney. New York: Random House, 1973.
- *The Little Igloo* by Lorraine and Jerrold Beim. Illustrated by Howard Simon. New York: Harcourt, Brace and World, 1941.

NOTES:

© 1989 by Shirley A. Steinmetz

Level I

black

① all black on white

igloo

SILLY SCRIBBLE TEACHER-DIRECTED PAGE

Level II

LETTER RECOGNITION: I i
SILLY SCRIBBLE: ice cream cone (long I sound)
PAPER DIRECTION: "standing up"
STAR COLOR: brown

TEACHER DIRECTIONS: Look for the number 1. This will tell you where to make the START line and what color to use.

- Keep in mind the basic strokes described in Section 1.
- Always use the whole paper when doing Silly Scribbles.
- Always write the name of the Silly Scribble or encourage the children to try and write it themselves.
- Emphasize to the children that this is only one way of making an ice cream cone. Discuss other ways.

QUESTIONS YOU COULD ASK:
- What sound does "ice cream" begin with?
- How many scoops of ice cream did we make?
- What flavor are they?
- Color in the ice cream to look like your favorite kind.
- Can you tell or write what kind it is?

ADDITIONAL ACTIVITIES:
- Discuss how vowels have more than one sound.
- Have ice cream for a snack. Look at the edges of the ice cream. Try drawing the way it look.
- Discuss what happens to ice cream on a warm day.
- Discuss the many different flavors of ice cream.
- Make a graph of who likes chocolate, strawberry, or vanilla.
- Make a huge ice cream cone out of paper. Let the children cut out a "scoop" of ice cream. They can color it in and write what flavor it is. Stack the scoops on top of the cone to make a huge ice cream cone.

CREATIVE THINKING STARTERS:
- Think up a silly name for a new ice cream. Draw what it would look like in a cone. How about "iguana green chip"?

SUGGESTED READING:
- *I Walk and Read* by Tana Hoban. New York: Greenwillow Books, 1984.

NOTES:

brown

8 black

7 black

6 black

① brown

2 brown

brown

5 brown

brown 4

3 brown

ice cream

Level II

SILLY SCRIBBLE TEACHER-DIRECTED PAGE

Level III

LETTER RECOGNITION: I i
SILLY SCRIBBLE: iguana
PAPER DIRECTION: "lying down"
STAR COLOR: brown

TEACHER DIRECTIONS: Look for the number 1. This will tell you where to make the START line and what color to use.

- Keep in mind the basic strokes described in Section 1.
- Always use the whole paper when doing Silly Scribbles.
- Always write the name of the Silly Scribble or encourage the children to try and write it themselves.
- Emphasize to the children that this is only one way of making an iguana. Discuss other ways.

QUESTIONS YOU COULD ASK:
- What sound does "iguana" begin with?
- Where is this iguana?
- What do you think the iguana will eat?
- Looking at this Silly Scribble, how did the iguana get up the tree?

ADDITIONAL ACTIVITIES:
- Can you show me how an iguana moves around on the ground?
- Do you think you would like an iguana for a pet?

CREATIVE THINKING STARTERS:
- Compare pictures of an iguana to a dinosaur. How are they alike and different?

SUGGESTED READING:
- *Me Too Iguana* by Jacquelyn Reinach. Illustrated by Richard Hefter. New York: Holt, Rinehart and Winston, 1977.

NOTES:

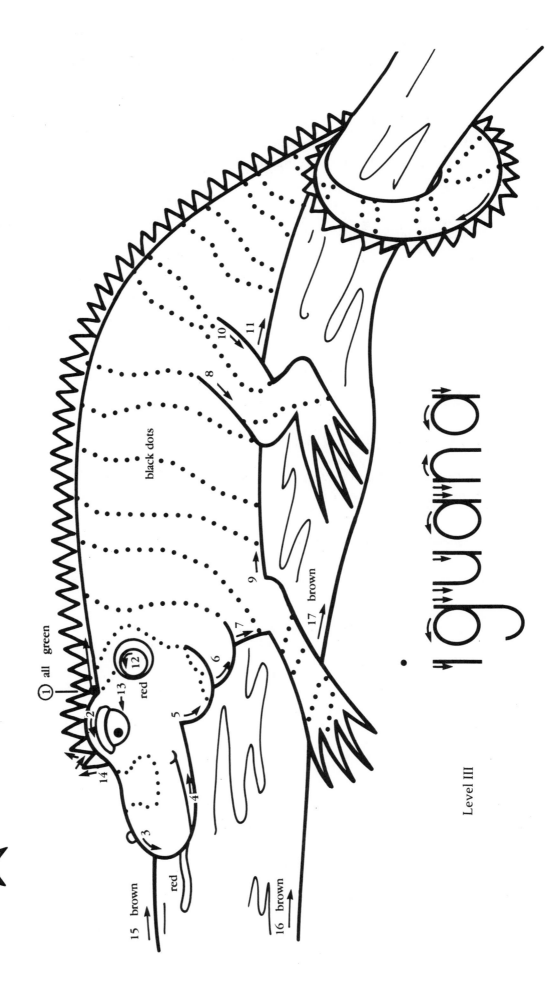

© 1989 by Shirley A. Steinmetz

brown

iguana

Level III

black dots

all green

red

red

brown

brown

brown

SILLY SCRIBBLE TEACHER-DIRECTED PAGE

Level I

LETTER RECOGNITION: J j
SILLY SCRIBBLE: jump rope
PAPER DIRECTION: "lying down"
STAR COLOR: red

TEACHER DIRECTIONS: Look for the number 1. This will tell you where to make the START line and what color to use.

- Keep in mind the basic strokes described in Section 1.
- Always use the whole paper when doing Silly Scribbles.
- Always write the name of the Silly Scribble or encourage the children to try and write it themselves.
- Emphasize to the children that this is only one way of making a jump rope. Discuss other ways.

QUESTIONS YOU COULD ASK:
- What sound does "jump rope" begin with?
- What pattern do you see?

ADDITIONAL ACTIVITIES:
- Share jump rope "sayings."
- Discuss compound words.
- Make a list of other action words like "jump." Then see if you can do it.
- Let the children try using a jump rope by themselves and with friends.

CREATIVE THINKING STARTERS:
- Think of other uses for a jump rope. What would it be called? A "hop rope"?
- Use a jump rope and make it form different shapes (circles, triangle, rectangle, oval, and so forth.) Then play a "guess the shape" game with the rope.

SUGGESTED READING:
- *The Whim-Wham Book* collected by Duncan Emrich. Illustrated by Ib Ohlsson. New York: Four Winds Press, 1975, pages 100-104.
- *The Hodgepodge Book* collected by Duncan Emrich. Illustrated by Ib Ohlsson. New York: Four Winds Press, 1972, pages 251-252.

NOTES:

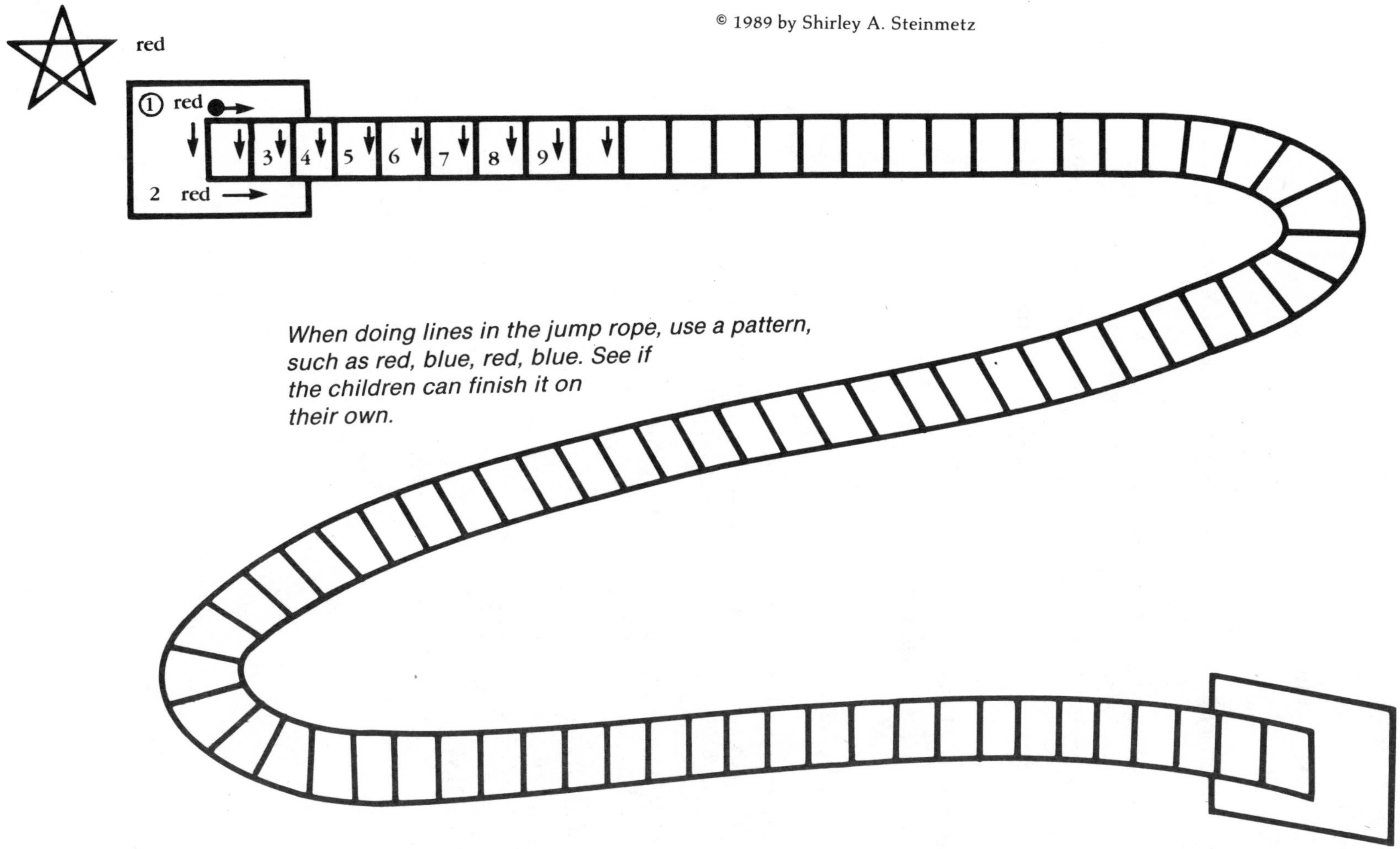

When doing lines in the jump rope, use a pattern, such as red, blue, red, blue. See if the children can finish it on their own.

red

① red •

2 red →

3 4 5 6 7 8 9

j u m p r o p e

Level I

SILLY SCRIBBLE TEACHER-DIRECTED PAGE

Level II

LETTER RECOGNITION: J j
SILLY SCRIBBLE: jacket
PAPER DIRECTION: "standing up"
STAR COLOR: blue

TEACHER DIRECTIONS: Look for the number 1. This will tell you where to make the START line and what color to use.

- Keep in mind the basic strokes described in Section 1.
- Always use the whole paper when doing Silly Scribbles.
- Always write the name of the Silly Scribble or encourage the children to try and write it themselves.
- Emphasize to the children that this is only one way of making a jacket. Discuss other ways.

QUESTIONS YOU COULD ASK:

- What sound does "jacket" begin with?
- How many buttons does it have?

ADDITIONAL ACTIVITIES:

- Discuss jackets. Have each child get his or her jacket and sort the jackets into different piles (by color, texture, and so forth).
- Have the children draw a picture of themselves in their jacket.
- Put all of the jackets into a pile and see if the children can find their own without touching another person.
- Graph jackets by fasteners, buttons, snaps, zippers, Velcro.
- Make a list of all the things that have pockets.

CREATIVE THINKING STARTERS:

- Do you think there is a difference between a jacket and a coat?
- Make a list of the things you could carry in a jacket pocket.

SUGGESTED READING:

- *There's a Wocket in My Pocket!* by Dr. Seuss. New York: Random House, 1974.

NOTES:

blue

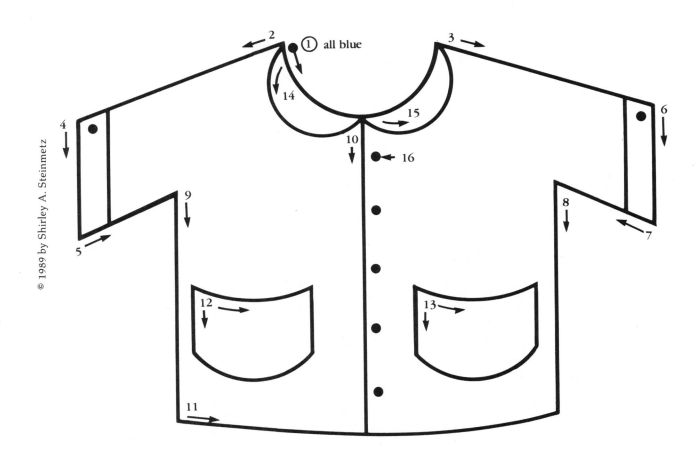

① all blue

jacket

Level II

SILLY SCRIBBLE TEACHER-DIRECTED PAGE

LETTER RECOGNITION: J j
SILLY SCRIBBLE: joey
PAPER DIRECTION: "standing up"
STAR COLOR: brown

TEACHER DIRECTIONS: Look for the number 1. This will tell you where to make the START line and what color to use.

- Keep in mind the basic strokes described in Section 1.
- Always use the whole paper when doing Silly Scribbles.
- Always write the name of the Silly Scribble or encourage the children to try and write it themselves.
- Emphasize to the children that this is only one way of making a joey. Discuss other ways.

QUESTIONS YOU COULD ASK:

- What sound does "joey" begin with?
- Where is the baby kangaroo?
- Have you ever seen a kangaroo with a joey in her pouch? (Males do not have pouches.)

ADDITIONAL ACTIVITIES:

- Make a list of things that have pockets.
- Make ten mother kangaroos with a number from 1 to 10 on each pouch. Have the children make joeys. Doing one at a time, encourage the children to put the correct number of joeys into each pouch.
- Can you jump like a kangaroo? How far can you jump?
- Get a copy of *National Geographic* that features kangaroos. Study the photos of the tiny newborn and the way it makes its way to its food.

CREATIVE THINKING STARTERS:

- If you were a joey, what do you think it would be like to ride in a pouch? What do you think would be the advantages of living in a pouch?

SUGGESTED READING:

- *Katy No-Pocket* by Emmy Payne. Illustrated by H. A. Rey. Boston: Houghton Mifflin, 1944.
- *What Do You Do With a Kangaroo?* by Mercer Mayer. New York: Four Winds Press, 1973.

NOTES:

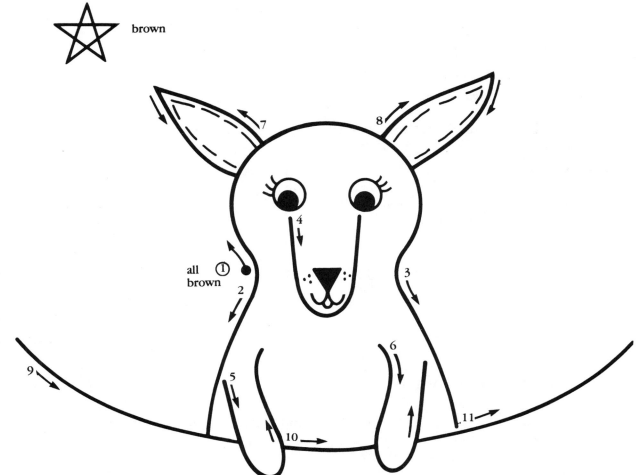

brown

all brown

① 2

3 4 5 6 7 8 9 10 11

joey

Level III

SILLY SCRIBBLE TEACHER-DIRECTED PAGE

Level I

LETTER RECOGNITION: K k
SILLY SCRIBBLE: kite
PAPER DIRECTION: "standing up"
STAR COLOR: blue

TEACHER DIRECTIONS: Look for the number 1. This will tell you where to make the START line and what color to use.

- Keep in mind the basic strokes described in Section 1.
- Always use the whole paper when doing Silly Scribbles.
- Always write the name of the Silly Scribble or encourage the children to try and write it themselves.
- Emphasize to the children that this is only one way of making a kite. Discuss other ways.

QUESTIONS YOU COULD ASK:
- What letter does "kite" begin with?
- What shape is the kite?
- What shape are the bows?
- What is the pattern of the bows?

ADDITIONAL ACTIVITIES:
- Make a kite and fly it.
- Pretend you are a kite flying in the wind. Now the wind has stopped blowing. What will you do?
- Make a list of words that rhyme with "kite."
- Number ten child-made kites with strings. Have the children attach the correct number of bows to match the number of strings on each kite.

CREATIVE THINKING STARTERS:
- Why does a kite need a tail? Have the children experiment with no tail, heavy, tail, very light tail, or unbalanced tail. Discuss what they discovered.

SUGGESTED READING:
- *The Emperor and the Kite* by Jane Yolen. Illustrated by Ed Young. Cleveland and New York: The World Publishing Co., 1967.

NOTES:

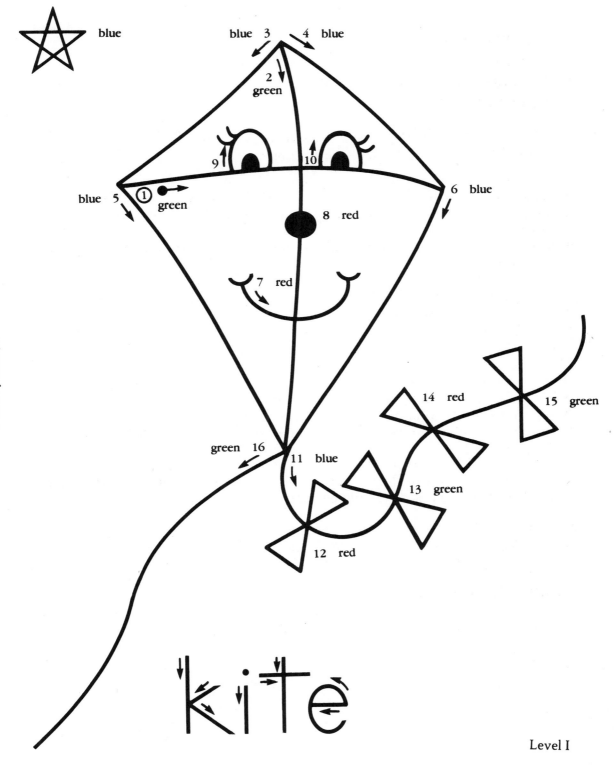

blue

blue 3   4 blue

2
green

9   10

blue 5   6 blue
① green

8 red

7 red

green 16   11 blue

14 red   15 green

13 green

12 red

kite

Level I

SILLY SCRIBBLE TEACHER-DIRECTED PAGE

LETTER RECOGNITION: K k
SILLY SCRIBBLE: koala
PAPER DIRECTION: "standing up"
STAR COLOR: green

TEACHER DIRECTIONS: Look for the number 1. This will tell you where to make the START line and what color to use.

- Keep in mind the basic strokes described in Section 1.
- Always use the whole paper when doing Silly Scribbles.
- Always write the name of the Silly Scribble or encourage the children to try and write it themselves.
- Emphasize to the children that this is only one way of making a koala. Discuss other ways.

QUESTIONS YOU COULD ASK:
- What sound does the word "koala" end with?
- Where is the koala?
- Do you know what kind of tree this is? (eucalyptus)

ADDITIONAL ACTIVITIES:
- Let the children paint a picture of a koala bear. Write or tell about their pictures.
- Watch a video or film or look at pictures about the koala. Discuss the things the children found interesting about the koala.

CREATIVE THINKING STARTERS:
- Since the koala sleeps during the day and is awake at night, try to imagine and discuss how your life would be different if you did that.

SUGGESTED READING:
- *Koala Bear Twins* by Inez Hogen. New York: E. P. Dutton, 1955.

NOTES:

Level II

SILLY SCRIBBLE TEACHER-DIRECTED PAGE

Level III

LETTER RECOGNITION: K k
SILLY SCRIBBLE: kiwi
PAPER DIRECTION: "lying down"
STAR COLOR: black

TEACHER DIRECTIONS: Look for the number 1. This will tell you where to make the START line and what color to use.

- Keep in mind the basic strokes described in Section 1.
- Always use the whole paper when doing Silly Scribbles.
- Always write the name of the Silly Scribble or encourage the children to try and write it themselves.
- Emphasize to the children that this is only one way of making a kiwi. Discuss other ways.

QUESTIONS YOU COULD ASK:
- What sound does the word "kiwi" begin with?
- Have you ever seen a kiwi?
- How big do you think a kiwi is? (slightly smaller than a chicken)

ADDITIONAL ACTIVITIES:
- Discuss the difference between this bird and kiwi fruit.
- Serve kiwi fruit for a snack.
- Find out more about the kiwi.
- Encourage the children to make ten different insects. Let the kiwi pretend to eat them one at a time to see what is left.
- Make a list of nighttime (nocturnal) birds and animals.

CREATIVE THINKING STARTERS:
- Did you know that there is a nostril at the very end of the kiwi's beak? It is the only bird that has one! What do you think a kiwi would do with a nostril? (smell for food) Pretend you are a kiwi, and you are smelling your favorite food. Share and discuss the many types of foods that you can tell just by smelling what it is.

SUGGESTED READING:
- *The Goodnight Circle* by Carolyn Lesser. New York: Harcourt Brace Jovanovich, 1984.
- *Birds Do the Strangest Things* by Lenora and Arthur Hornblow. Illustrations by Michael K. Frith. New York: Random House, 1965, page 18.

NOTES:

black

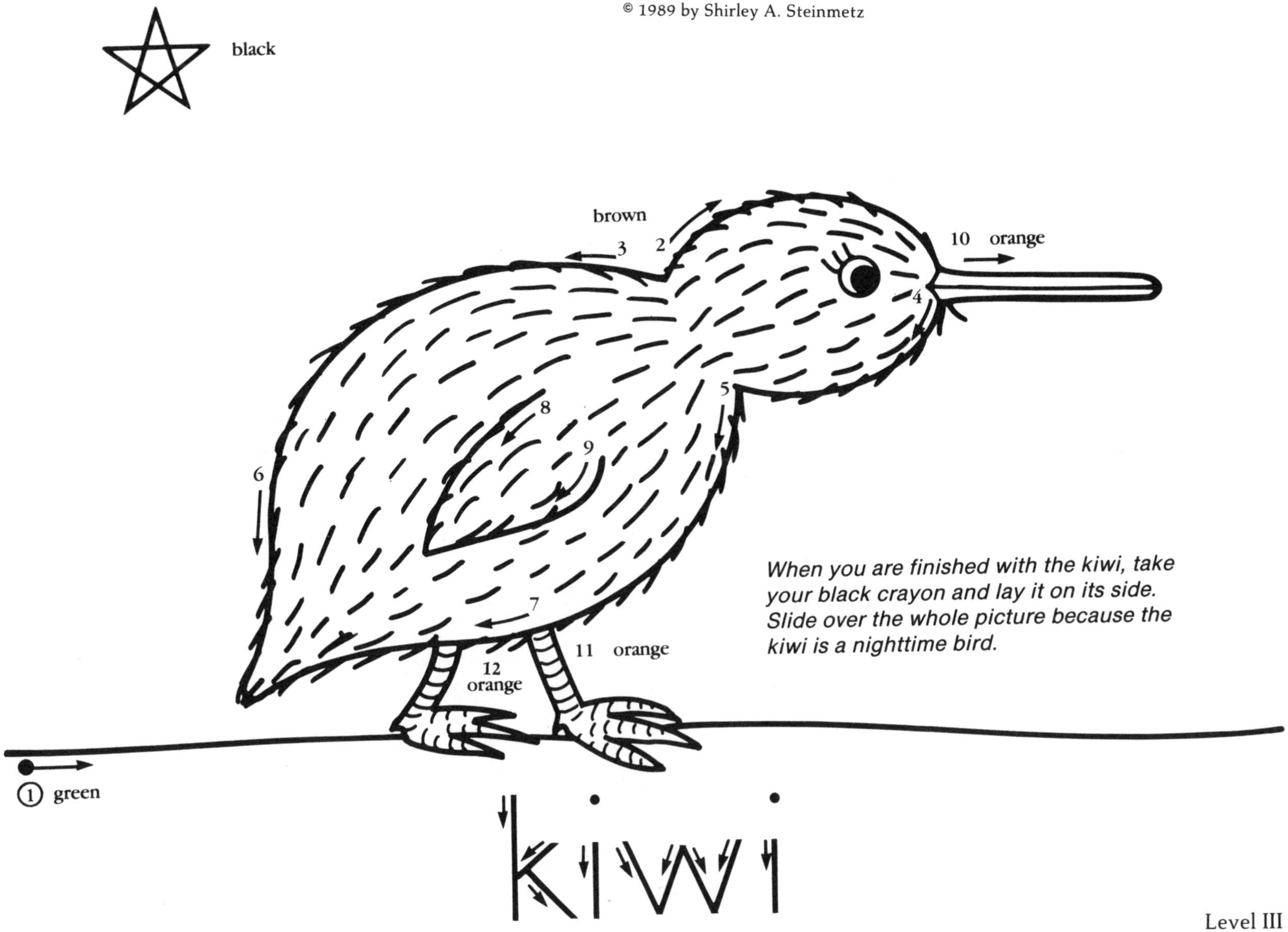

When you are finished with the kiwi, take your black crayon and lay it on its side. Slide over the whole picture because the kiwi is a nighttime bird.

brown

10 orange

11 orange

12 orange

green

KIWI

Level III

SILLY SCRIBBLE TEACHER-DIRECTED PAGE

Level I

LETTER RECOGNITION: L l
SILLY SCRIBBLE: lamb
PAPER DIRECTION: "lying down"
STAR COLOR: green

TEACHER DIRECTIONS: Look for the number 1. This will tell you where to make the START line and what color to use.

- Keep in mind the basic strokes described in Section 1.
- Always use the whole paper when doing Silly Scribbles.
- Always write the name of the Silly Scribble or encourage the children to try and write it themselves.
- Emphasize to the children that this is only one way of making a lamb. Discuss other ways.

QUESTIONS YOU COULD ASK:
- What sound does "lamb" begin with?
- What color is this lamb?
- What other colors do lambs come in?
- What shape is the lamb's body?

ADDITIONAL ACTIVITIES:
- Play "Little Lost Lamb." One child goes out of the room and is the shepherd. One other child (the "lamb") hides. When the shepherd comes back into the room, the children give the shepherd clues to tell which lamb is missing. When the shepherd guesses correctly, the lamb comes out of hiding saying "Baa." The lamb then gets to be the shepherd.
- Visit a farm in the spring to see baby lambs.
- Discuss wool and how it is made.
- Discuss March "coming in like a lion or a lamb."

CREATIVE THINKING STARTERS:
- Would you like a lamb for a pet? Where would you keep it? What would you feed it?

SUGGESTED READING:
- *The Little Lamb* by Judy Dunn. Photographs by Phoebe Dunn. New York: Random House, 1977.

NOTES:

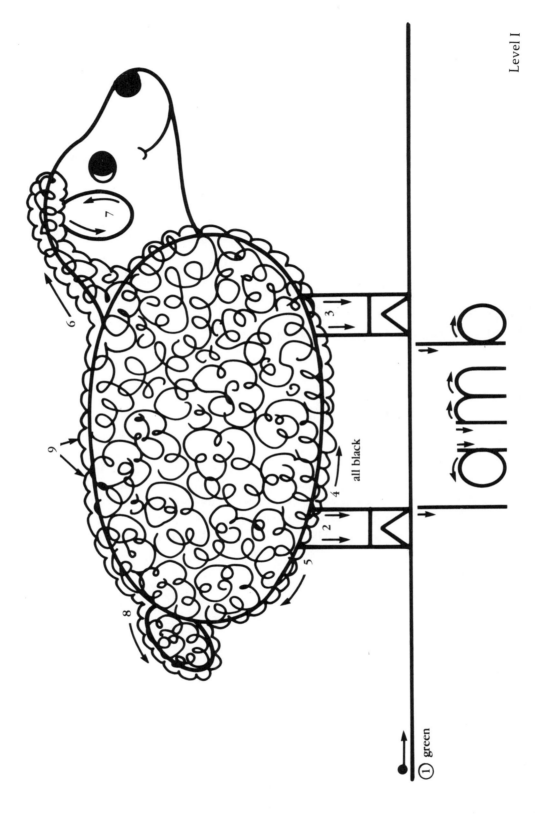

© 1989 by Shirley A. Steinmetz

green

Level I

all black

l ă m b

① green

SILLY SCRIBBLE TEACHER-DIRECTED PAGE

Level II

LETTER RECOGNITION: L l
SILLY SCRIBBLE: lighthouse
PAPER DIRECTION: "standing up"
STAR COLOR: blue

TEACHER DIRECTIONS: Look for the number 1. This will tell you where to make the START line and what color to use.

• Keep in mind the basic strokes described in Section 1.
• Always use the whole paper when doing Silly Scribbles.
• Always write the name of the Silly Scribble or encourage the children to try and write it themselves.
• Emphasize to the children that this is only one way of making a lighthouse. Discuss other ways.

QUESTIONS YOU COULD ASK:
• What sound does "lighthouse" begin with?
• Where would you find a lighthouse?
• What shape are the windows?

ADDITIONAL ACTIVITIES:
• Discuss what a lighthouse does and why they are necessary.
• Can you think of a time other than at night when a lighthouse would have its lights on?
• Discuss compound words. Have the children make up some picture riddles of compound words (hotdog, watchman, pitchfork, and the like).
• Find pictures of ancient lighthouses and discuss them. Locate them on a map.
• Since the sun is a great source of light, make solar prints by laying objects on pieces of construction paper and setting them in the sun. Observe what happens.

CREATIVE THINKING STARTERS:
• How many different science experiments can you find that use "light"? Share, experiment, and discuss with the children.

SUGGESTED READING:
• *The Little Red Lighthouse and the Great Grey Bridge* by Hildegarde H. Swift and Lynd Ward. New York: Harcourt, Brace, and World, 1942.

NOTES:

blue

black
10

red 8

yellow
11

9 red

yellow

7
black

6

red 4

5 red

12
black

13 black

14 black

brown

2 black

15

① black

3 blue

black

black

black

black

© 1989 by Shirley A. Steinmetz

lighthouse

Level II

SILLY SCRIBBLE TEACHER-DIRECTED PAGE

Level III

LETTER RECOGNITION: L l
SILLY SCRIBBLE: llama
PAPER DIRECTION: "standing up"
STAR COLOR: blue

TEACHER DIRECTIONS: Look for the number 1. This will tell you where to make the START line and what color to use.

- Keep in mind the basic strokes described in Section 1.
- Always use the whole paper when doing Silly Scribbles.
- Always write the name of the Silly Scribble or encourage the children to try and write it themselves.
- Emphasize to the children that this is only one way of making a llama. Discuss other ways.

QUESTIONS YOU COULD ASK:
- What sound does "llama" begin with?
- Why do you think a llama has so much fur?
- What line did you make first?

ADDITIONAL ACTIVITIES:
- Discuss why a llama would make a good pet.
- Make up a collaborative silly story about the "Mammá Llama from the Bahamas."

CREATIVE THINKING STARTERS:
- What reasons can you think of to tell why a llama spits?

NOTES:

blue

all brown

12

①

3

4

11

2

13   make "furry"

5

10

9

7

6

8

Llama

Level III

SILLY SCRIBBLE TEACHER-DIRECTED PAGE

Level I

LETTER RECOGNITION: M m
SILLY SCRIBBLE: monkey
PAPER DIRECTION: "standing up"
STAR COLOR: red

TEACHER DIRECTIONS: Look for the number 1. This will tell you where to make the START line and what color to use.

- Keep in mind the basic strokes described in Section 1.
- Always use the whole paper when doing Silly Scribbles.
- Always write the name of the Silly Scribble or encourage the children to try and write it themselves.
- Emphasize to the children that this is only one way of making a monkey. Discuss other ways.

QUESTIONS YOU COULD ASK:
- Where is the monkey's face?
- Why do you think the monkey has its back to you?
- Do you know what monkeys use their tails for?
- What is the monkey holding?

ADDITIONAL ACTIVITIES:
- Pretend you are a monkey. What sound would you make? How would you walk?
- Visit a zoo and watch the monkeys.
- Paint or cut and paste a monkey. Show it doing something funny.
- Read *Caps for Sale* and act it out, letting one child be the salesperson and the rest be the monkeys in the tree. Let the children take turns being the person who sells the hats.

CREATIVE THINKING STARTERS:
- What is "monkey business"? Make up a story about "monkey business."

SUGGESTED READING:
- Read any of the *Curious George* stories written by H. A. Rey.
- *Caps for Sale* by Esphyr Slobodkin. New York: Scholastic, 1984.

NOTES:

red

make the monkey fuzzy

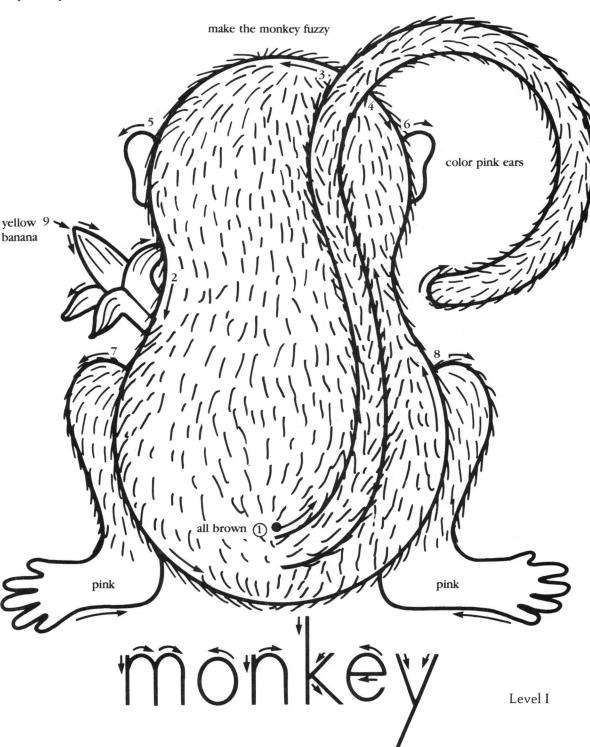

color pink ears

yellow 9
banana

all brown ①

pink

pink

© 1989 by Shirley A. Steinmetz

monkey

Level I

SILLY SCRIBBLE TEACHER-DIRECTED PAGE

Level II

LETTER RECOGNITION: M m
SILLY SCRIBBLE: moose
PAPER DIRECTION: "lying down"
STAR COLOR: brown

TEACHER DIRECTIONS: Look for the number 1. This will tell you where to make the START line and what color to use.

- Keep in mind the basic strokes described in Section 1.
- Always use the whole paper when doing Silly Scribbles.
- Always write the name of the Silly Scribble or encourage the children to try and write it themselves.
- Emphasize to the children that this is only one way of making a moose. Discuss other ways.

QUESTIONS YOU COULD ASK:

- When did you realize that it was a moose?
- Where is the rest of the moose?
- Why do you think a moose has such big antlers?

ADDITIONAL ACTIVITIES:

- Make a list of words that rhyme with "moose."
- Make a list of all animals you can that have antlers.
- Help the children make chocolate mousse for a snack. Combine 5 tablespoons cold water and 1 cup semisweet chocolate chips. Place over medium heat and melt. Mix with 5 beaten egg yolks. Add 1 teaspoon vanilla. Beat 5 egg whites until stiff, and fold into the chocolate mixture. Spoon mixture into small paper cups. Chill. Top with a little whipped cream.

CREATIVE THINKING STARTERS:

- Make a moose hat. Let the children try it on and discuss the silly things that would happen if they had antlers like a moose.

SUGGESTED READING:

- *Thidwick the Big-hearted Moose* by Dr. Seuss. New York: Random House, 1948.
- *The Moose Is Loose* by Mike Thaler. Illustrated by Toni Goffe. New York: Scholastic Book Service, 1980.
- *Morris Has a Cold* by Bernard Wiseman. New York: Scholastic Book Services, 1977.

NOTES:

Level II

4

12

6

8

2

9

10

3

5

7

① all brown

11

brown

mōōse

SILLY SCRIBBLE TEACHER-DIRECTED PAGE

Level III

LETTER RECOGNITION: M m
SILLY SCRIBBLE: merry-go-round
PAPER DIRECTION: "lying down"
STAR COLOR: purple

TEACHER DIRECTIONS: Look for the number 1. This will tell you where to make the START line and what color to use.

- Keep in mind the basic strokes described in Section 1.
- Always use the whole paper when doing Silly Scribbles.
- Always write the name of the Silly Scribble or encourage the children to try and write it themselves.
- Emphasize to the children that this is only one way of making a merry-go-round. Discuss other ways.

QUESTIONS YOU COULD ASK:

- What was your first clue that this was a merry-go-round?
- How many horses are on the merry-go-round?
- Have you ever ridden a merry-go-round?

ADDITIONAL ACTIVITIES:

- After looking at pictures of the ornate horses that are on a merry-go-round, let the children each paint a large horse for a merry-go-round. Then use these on a bulletin board to construct a brightly colored class merry-go-round.
- Discuss how the horses move on a merry-go-round. Pretend you are on a merry-go-round and move around in a circle with alternating children moving up and down on the pretend horses. Play appropriate music.

CREATIVE THINKING STARTERS:

- Share ideas about the merry-go-round horse that ran away. Write a collaborative story.

SUGGESTED READING:

- *Merry-Go-Round* by Oretta Leigh. Illustrated by Kathryn E. Shoemaker. New York: Holiday, 1985.
- *Carousel* by David Crews. New York: Greenwillow Books, 1982.

NOTES:

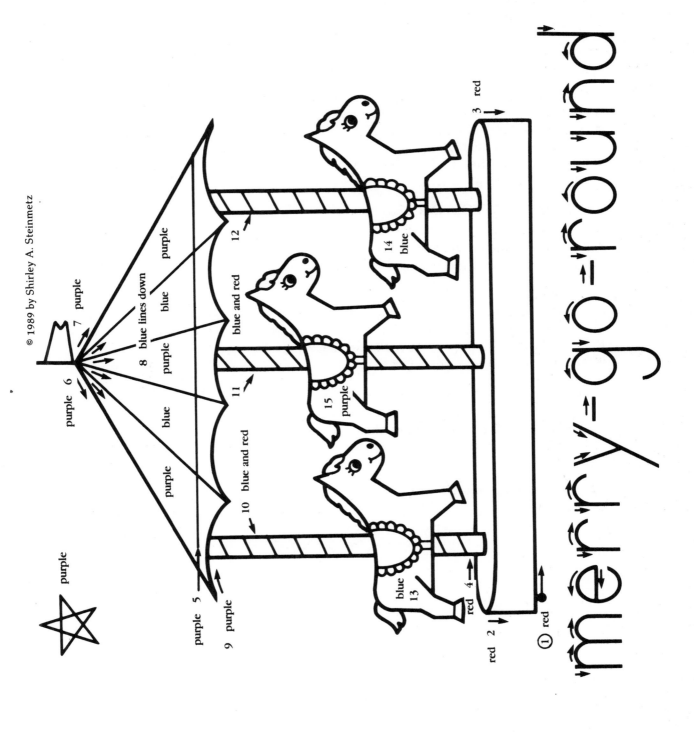

© 1989 by Shirley A. Steinmetz

Level III

me̊rry-go-r̄ound

SILLY SCRIBBLE TEACHER-DIRECTED PAGE

Level I

LETTER RECOGNITION: N n
SILLY SCRIBBLE: necklace
PAPER DIRECTION: "standing up"
STAR COLOR: blue

TEACHER DIRECTIONS: Look for the number 1. This will tell you where to make the START line and what color to use.

- Keep in mind the basic strokes described in Section 1.
- Always use the whole paper when doing Silly Scribbles.
- Always write the name of the Silly Scribble or encourage the children to try and write it themselves.
- Emphasize to the children that this is only one way of making a necklace. Discuss other ways.

QUESTIONS YOU COULD ASK:

- What sound does "necklace" begin with?
- Do you see a pattern? What is it?
- Who could wear this necklace?

ADDITIONAL ACTIVITIES:

- Have a necklace day during which everyone has to wear a necklace. Sort the necklaces according to color, length, material, etc.
- String beads in a pattern to make necklaces.
- String cereal to make necklaces.

CREATIVE THINKING STARTERS:

- Make a "children" necklace. Have the children form a circle by holding hands. See how many different ways they can arrange themselves to make a pattern in their giant necklace. Standing, sitting? Boy, girl? Hands up, hands down? Color of hair, clothes, kinds of shoes, etc.

SUGGESTED READING:

- *Shapes and Things* by Tana Hoban. New York: Macmillan Publishing Company, 1970.

NOTES:

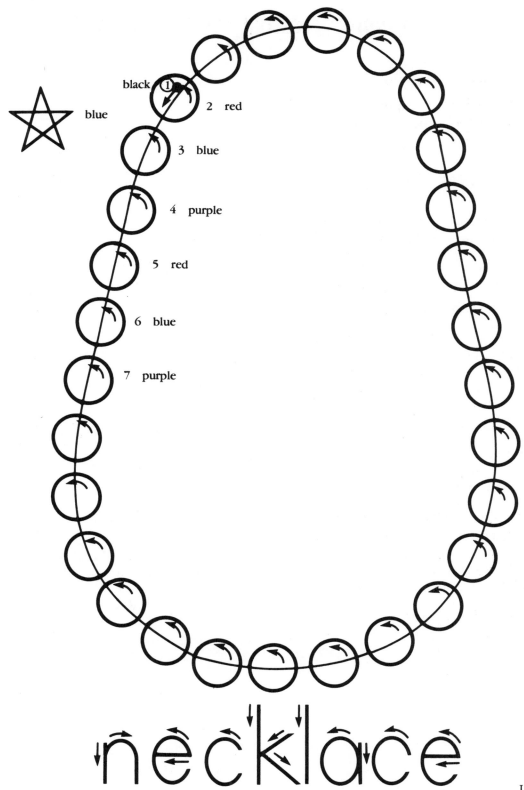

blue

black ①
2 red
3 blue
4 purple
5 red
6 blue
7 purple

necklace

Level I

SILLY SCRIBBLE TEACHER-DIRECTED PAGE

Level II

LETTER RECOGNITION: N n
SILLY SCRIBBLE: numbers
PAPER DIRECTION: "lying down"
STAR COLOR: brown

TEACHER DIRECTIONS: Look for the number 1. This will tell you where to make the START line and what color to use.

- Keep in mind the basic strokes described in Section 1.
- Always use the whole paper when doing Silly Scribbles.

QUESTIONS YOU COULD ASK:
- What are these called?
- Whenever you make a number, ask the children to tell you what it is.
- When you are finished making the numbers, ask the children to make whatever they want in each box to show the amount. (For example, 2 fish? 8 apples? 7 circles?)

ADDITIONAL ACTIVITIES:
- Have children take turns writing numbers on the chalkboard. The other children try to identify the numbers.
- The list is endless . . . check with your school's math program and have fun!

CREATIVE THINKING STARTERS:
- How high can you count?

SUGGESTED READING:
- *The Count Counts a Party* by Judy Freudberg and Tony Geiss. Illustrated by Tom Cooke. Featuring Jim Henson's Sesame Street Muppets. New York: Western Publising Company, 1980.
- *The Ten-Alarm Camp-out* by Cathy Warren. Illustrated by Steven Kellogg. New York: Lothrop, Lee and Shepard, 1983.

NOTES:

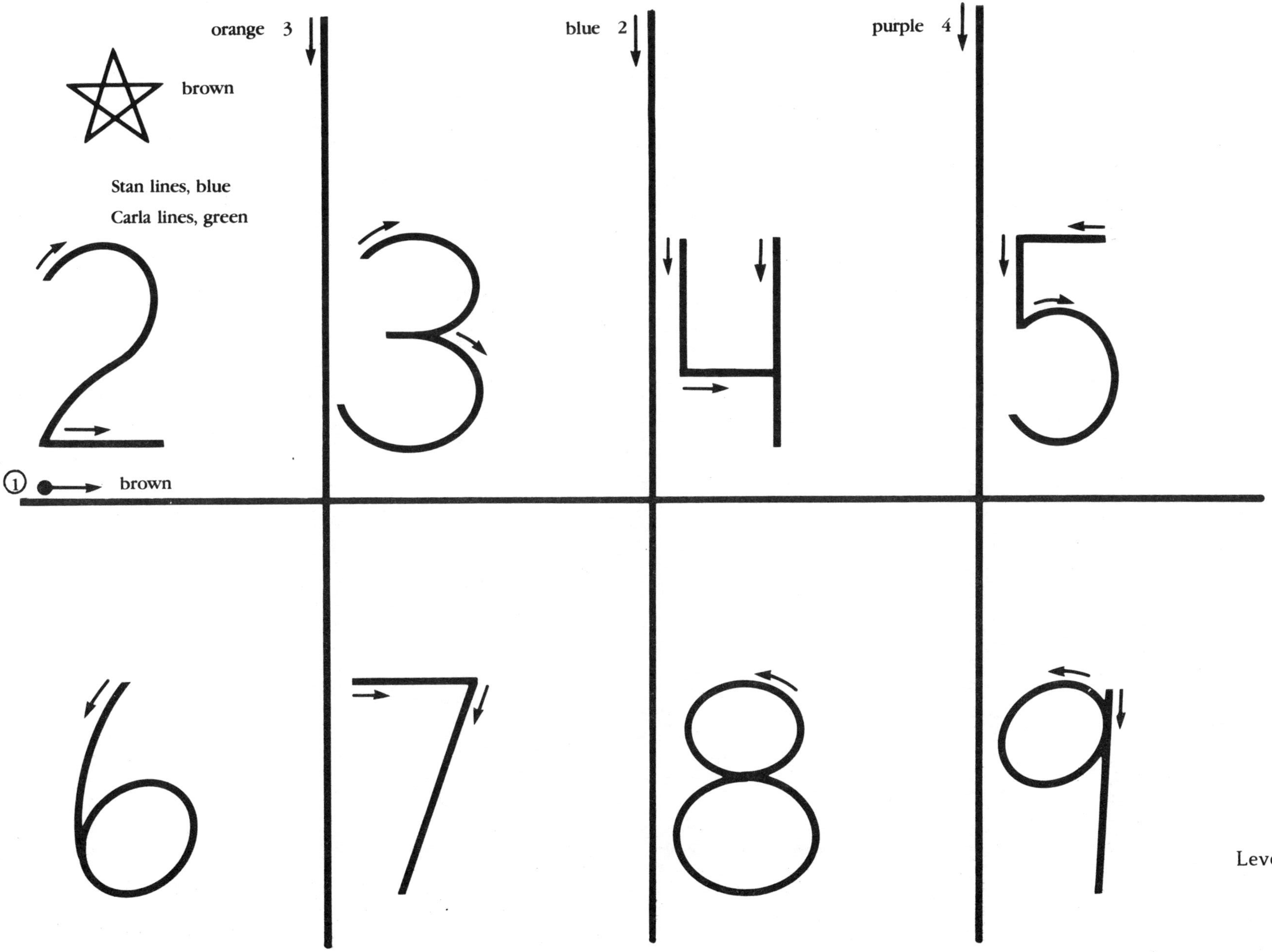
orange 3
blue 2
purple 4
brown
Stan lines, blue
Carla lines, green
1
brown
2
3
4
5
6
7
8
9

Level II

SILLY SCRIBBLE TEACHER-DIRECTED PAGE

LETTER RECOGNITION: N n
SILLY SCRIBBLE: nest (stork's)
PAPER DIRECTION: "standing up"
STAR COLOR: blue

TEACHER DIRECTIONS: Look for the number 1. This will tell you where to make the START line and what color to use.

- Keep in mind the basic strokes described in Section 1.
- Always use the whole paper when doing Silly Scribbles.
- Always write the name of the Silly Scribble or encourage the children to try and write it themselves.
- Emphasize to the children that this is only one way of making a nest. Discuss other ways.

QUESTIONS YOU COULD ASK:

- Where has the bird built this nest?
- Do you know what bird built this nest?

ADDITIONAL ACTIVITIES:

- Discuss the different things a bird needs to build a nest.
- Pretend you are an egg in a nest. You are starting to crack. How will you get out of the egg? What kind of bird are you?
- Make a list of all the birds the children know.
- Explore the different kinds of nests that birds build.

CREATIVE THINKING STARTERS:

- Encourage each child to create (invent) his or her own personal nest. What materials would you use? Provide mud, small twigs, straw, strings, clay, Styrofoam, and anything else you or the children can think of.

SUGGESTED READING:

- *Horton Hatches the Egg* by Dr. Seuss. New York: Random House, 1940.

NOTES:

blue

10   blue

brown sticks

9
brown

red ①

3   red

2   red

4   red

5   red

6   red

7   red

red   8

11   blue

nest

Level III

SILLY SCRIBBLE TEACHER-DIRECTED PAGE

Level I

LETTER RECOGNITION:　O o
SILLY SCRIBBLE:　octopus
PAPER DIRECTION:　"lying down"
STAR COLOR:　blue

TEACHER DIRECTIONS: Look for the number 1. This will tell you where to make the START line and what color to use.

- Keep in mind the basic strokes described in Section 1.
- Always use the whole paper when doing Silly Scribbles.
- Always write the name of the Silly Scribble or encourage the children to try and write it themselves.
- Making each arm a different color helps the children with sequence and placement.
- Emphasize to the children that this is only one way of making an octopus. Discuss other ways.

QUESTIONS YOU COULD ASK:
- How many legs does an octopus have?
- Where does an octopus live?
- What sound does "octopus" begin with?

ADDITIONAL ACTIVITIES:
- Take a trip to an aquarium.
- Make a large octopus with eight legs, with a number on each leg. Have the children make eight fish with dots on the sides to match the numbers on the legs. Play "Put the Fish on the Octopus" and see if the children can put the correct fish on the correct leg.

CREATIVE THINKING STARTERS:
- Would you want to have eight arms? Why? What would you do?

SUGGESTED READING:
- *I Was All Thumbs* by Bernard Waber. Boston: Houghton Mifflin Company, 1975.

NOTES:

octopus

SILLY SCRIBBLE TEACHER-DIRECTED PAGE

Level II

LETTER RECOGNITION: O o
SILLY SCRIBBLE: owl
PAPER DIRECTION: "standing up"
STAR COLOR: black

TEACHER DIRECTIONS: Look for the number 1. This will tell you where to make the START line and what color to use.

- Keep in mind the basic strokes described in Section 1.
- Always use the whole paper when doing Silly Scribbles.
- Always write the name of the Silly Scribble or encourage the children to try and write it themselves.
- Emphasize to the children that this is only one way of making an owl. Discuss other ways.

QUESTIONS YOU COULD ASK:
- What does an owl say?
- How many circles do you see?
- Where do you see a pattern?

ADDITIONAL ACTIVITIES:
- Pretend you are an owl asleep on a branch. What time of day is it? Now the sun is setting, and it is time to fly away to look for supper. What will you eat? Where will you go?

CREATIVE THINKING STARTERS:
- Play "Guess whooo?" One child gets to be the owl. The owl gives one clue about another child in the room. "This person has brown hair. Guess whooo?" The other children make predictions. If no one guesses, the owl gives another clue. "This person has brown hair and blue eyes. Guess whooo?" The owl continues to give clues until someone guesses who. The child who guesses becomes the next owl. (Or you may want to give each child a chance to be the new owl.)

SUGGESTED READING:
- *Owl at Home* by Arnold Lobel. New York: Harper and Row Junior Books, 1975.
- *Owls* by Herbert S. Zim. Illustrated by James Gordon Irving. New York: William Morrow and Company, 1950.
- *Good-Night, Owl!* by Pat Hutchins. New York: Macmillan Publishing Company, 1972.

NOTES:

black

brown 11

① brown

brown 12

brown

black

who-o-o-o

orange

brown 4

brown 2

brown

5 brown

13 orange

3 brown

14 brown

15 orange

16 brown

brown 6

brown 7

17 orange

8 brown

18 black

orange 9

10 orange

19 black

OWL

Level II

SILLY SCRIBBLE TEACHER-DIRECTED PAGE

Level III

LETTER RECOGNITION: O o
SILLY SCRIBBLE: otter (sea otter)
PAPER DIRECTION: "lying down"
STAR COLOR: blue

TEACHER DIRECTIONS: Look for the number 1. This will tell you where to make the START line and what color to use.

- Keep in mind the basic strokes described in Section 1.
- Always use the whole paper when doing Silly Scribbles.
- Always write the name of the Silly Scribble or encourage the children to try and write it themselves.
- Emphasize to the children that this is only one way of making an otter. Discuss other ways.
- NOTE: When doing this Silly Scribble, start with the paper "lying down" to write the name and do some blue waves. Have the children turn their paper to "standing up" because the otter is easier to do that way. But when you go to write the word "otter," turn the paper back to "lying down." This way, the otter will float in the water to eat its snack.

QUESTIONS YOU COULD ASK:
- What sound does "otter" end with?
- What is the otter's snack going to be? (clam)

ADDITIONAL ACTIVITIES:
- Discuss what the otter might do with the shell after it has finished eating the clam inside. Have the children bring shells from home to start a class shell collection. Sort them according to size, color, or kind. Make a pattern of shells or glue them down to create a shell mosaic.

CREATIVE THINKING STARTERS:
- Discuss "floating." Set up a tub and a variety of things to float or sink. Make a list of those that float.

SUGGESTED READING:
- *Oscar Otter* by Nathaniel Benchley. Illustrated by Arnold Lobel. New York: Harper & Row, 1966.
- *Otter Swims* by Derek Hall. Illustrated by John Butler. New York: Sierra Club, Alfred A. Knopf, 1984.

NOTES:

otter

all brown ① black

black clam

blue blue blue blue blue blue

Level III

SILLY SCRIBBLE TEACHER-DIRECTED PAGE

Level I

LETTER RECOGNITION: P p
SILLY SCRIBBLE: panda
PAPER DIRECTIONS: "standing up"
STAR COLOR: black

TEACHER DIRECTIONS: Look for the number 1. This will tell you where to make the START line and what color to use.

- Keep in mind the basic strokes described in Section 1.
- Always use the whole paper when doing Silly Scribbles.
- Always write the name of the Silly Scribble or encourage the children to try and write it themselves.
- Emphasize to the children that this is only one way of making a panda. Discuss other ways.

QUESTIONS YOU COULD ASK:
- What sound does "panda" begin with? End with?
- Do you know what the plant is called? (bamboo)

ADDITIONAL ACTIVITIES:
- If you live near a zoo that has a panda, visit it.
- Make "Panda Pudding" for snack. Layer chocolate and vanilla puddings in a cup.
- Have "Panda Day." Have the children wear black and white. Make panda headbands with ears attached and make up the children's faces to look like panda bears. (Get written permission from parents before putting any makeup on a child in case of allergies.) Have a Panda Parade and take photos for later enjoyment and sharing.

CREATIVE THINKING STARTERS:
- Bring in some bamboo and discuss the many uses. Let the children experiment with floating, blowing bubbles, and so forth.

SUGGESTED READING:
- *A Book About Pandas* by Ruth Belov Gross. New York: Scholastic Book Services, 1980.
- *When Panda Came to Our House* by Helen Zane Jensen. New York: Dial Books for Young Readers, 1985.
- *Poppy the Panda* by Dick Gackenbach. New York: Clarion Books/Ticknor and Fields, 1984.

NOTES:

black

all black

10

11

green
bamboo

13   2

12

3

fill in
the black

4   5

6   8

7   9

panda

Level I

SILLY SCRIBBLE TEACHER-DIRECTED PAGE

LETTER RECOGNITION: P p
SILLY SCRIBBLE: penguin
PAPER DIRECTIONS: "standing up"
STAR COLOR: black

TEACHER DIRECTIONS: Look for the number 1. This will tell you where to make the START line and what color to use.

- Keep in mind the basic strokes described in Section 1.
- Always use the whole paper when doing Silly Scribbles.
- Always write the name of the Silly Scribble or encourage the children to try and write it themselves.
- Emphasize to the children that this is only one way of making a penguin. Discuss other ways.

QUESTIONS YOU COULD ASK:
- What kind of bird is this?
- Where does it live?
- What is the penguin holding? Do you think a real penguin could hold a fish? Why not?
- What sound does "penguin" begin with?
- Did you know that the daddy emperor penguin is the one who keeps the egg warm by holding it on his feet and covering it with his tummy? He does this for two months without eating.
- Which is the largest penguin?

ADDITIONAL ACTIVITIES:
- Pretend you are a penguin. How would you walk?
- Let the children look at photographs of penguins. Then ask them to paint or cut and paste their own penguin. Have the children tell or write about their picture.

CREATIVE THINKING STARTERS:
- Can a penguin fly? Why do you think nature has made this happen?

SUGGESTED READING:
- *Penguin Day* by Victoria Winteringham. New York: Harper & Row, 1982.
- *The Penguin That Hated the Cold* adapted by Barbara Brenner from Walt Disney. New York: Random House, 1973.

NOTES:

black

all
black

orange

① 2

3 4

10

5   11
blue   6

7

8 orange   orange 9

penguin

Level II

SILLY SCRIBBLE TEACHER-DIRECTED PAGE

Level III

LETTER RECOGNITION: P p
SILLY SCRIBBLE: parrot
PAPER DIRECTION: "standing up"
STAR COLOR: blue

TEACHER DIRECTIONS: Look for the number 1. This will tell you where to make the START line and what color to use.

- Keep in mind the basic strokes described in Section 1.
- Always use the whole paper when doing Silly Scribbles.
- Always write the name of the Silly Scribble or encourage the children to try and write it themselves.
- Emphasize to the children that this is only one way of making a parrot. Discuss other ways.

QUESTIONS YOU COULD ASK:
- What kind of bird is this?
- What sound does "parrot" begin with? End with?
- What was the second line you made?
- By looking at this Silly Scribble, are there more Stan lines or Carla lines?

ADDITIONAL ACTIVITIES:
- If you know anyone who has a parrot, invite that person to come and tell about his or her pet. If the parrot is polite, perhaps it could come, too. Encourage the children to ask questions.
- Share with the children your experience of a time when you have seen a parrot.
- Let the children paint a parrot. Write or tell about the pictures and make a parrot book in the shape of a parrot or a cracker.

CREATIVE THINKING STARTERS:
- If you had a parrot and could teach it to talk, what would you teach it to say? (Other than "Polly, want a cracker?")

SUGGESTED READING:
- *No One Noticed Ralph* by Bonnie Bishop. Illustrated by Jack Kent. New York: Doubleday and Company, 1979.
- *Percy the Parrot Passes the Puck* by Wayne Carley. Illustrated by Art Cumings. Champaign, IL: Garrard Publishing Company, 1972.

NOTES:

blue

3 green

8 red

9 yellow

10 →

red

11

yellow

green 2

green ①

4 green

5 green

14 brown

15 brown

12 orange

13 orange

6

7

parrot

Level III

SILLY SCRIBBLE TEACHER-DIRECTED PAGE

Level I

LETTER RECOGNITION: Q q
SILLY SCRIBBLE: quilt   ("the friendship quilt")
PAPER DIRECTION: "lying down"
STAR COLOR: any color

TEACHER DIRECTIONS: Look for the number 1. This will tell you where to make the START line and what color to use.

- Keep in mind the basic strokes described in Section 1.
- Always use the whole paper when doing Silly Scribbles.
- Emphasize to the children that this is only one way of making a quilt pattern. Discuss other ways.
- NOTE: The page shows four different patterns you can use to make a section of your quilt. Use any combinations of colors you would like, but I suggest no more than four. Then carry that color theme throughout the quilt pattern. Each rectangle represents one 12" x 18" piece of paper. Have the children write their names on the back. When your whole class has made the pieces to the quilt, lay them out on the floor and decide how you want the quilt to look. Turn them over and, using masking tape, "sew" the quilt together. You may want to make a paper border to frame the quilt. Then hang it somewhere for all to see. The children love to watch it being put together and seeing where their piece has gone. Because every child has a piece in the quilt, it can be called the "Friendship Quilt."

ADDITIONAL ACTIVITIES:

- After going through the steps, let the children create their own quilt patterns. Hang them around the class quilt.
- See if you can get some examples of quilts to share with the children.
- Invite a "quilting bee" group to come and tell about what they do.
- Have a group of children collaborate on their own quilt. Discuss different themes. A fall quilt? A shapes quilt?

SUGGESTED READING:

- *Sam Johnson and the Blue Ribbon Quilt* by Lisa Campbell Ernst. New York: Lothrop, Lee and Shepard, 1983.
- *The Quilt* by Ann Jonas. New York: Greenwillow Books, 1984.
- *The Patchwork Quilt* by Valerie Flournoy. Illustration by Jerry Pinkney. New York: Dial Books for Young Readers, 1985.

NOTES:

Level I

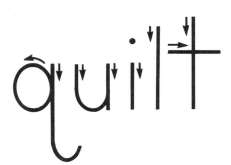

SILLY SCRIBBLE TEACHER-DIRECTED PAGE

Level II

LETTER RECOGNITION: Q q
SILLY SCRIBBLE: queen
PAPER DIRECTION: "standing up"
STAR COLOR: purple

TEACHER DIRECTIONS: Look for the number 1. This will tell you where to make the START line and what color to use.

- Keep in mind the basic strokes described in Section 1.
- Always use the whole paper when doing Silly Scribbles.
- Always write the name of the Silly Scribble or encourage the children to try and write it themselves.
- Emphasize to the children that this is only one way of making a queen. Discuss other ways.

QUESTIONS YOU COULD ASK:

- What sound does "queen" begin with? End with?
- Can you decorate the crown with jewels? (Supply sequins for the children.)
- What was the first line you made?
- Let the children finish the queen's face.

ADDITIONAL ACTIVITIES:

- Discuss how "Q" rarely goes anywhere without "u."
- Make crowns for the children and let them decorate to be kings and queens.
- Have the children design their own thrones.

CREATIVE THINKING STARTERS:

- If you were a queen (or king), what are some of the rules you would have?

SUGGESTED READING:

- *The Queen Who Couldn't Bake Gingerbread* by Dorothy Van Woerkom. Illustrated by Paul Galdone. New York: Alfred A. Knopf, 1975.
- *Her Majesty, Aunt Essie* by Amy Schwartz. Scarsdale, NY: Bradbury Press, 1984.

NOTES:

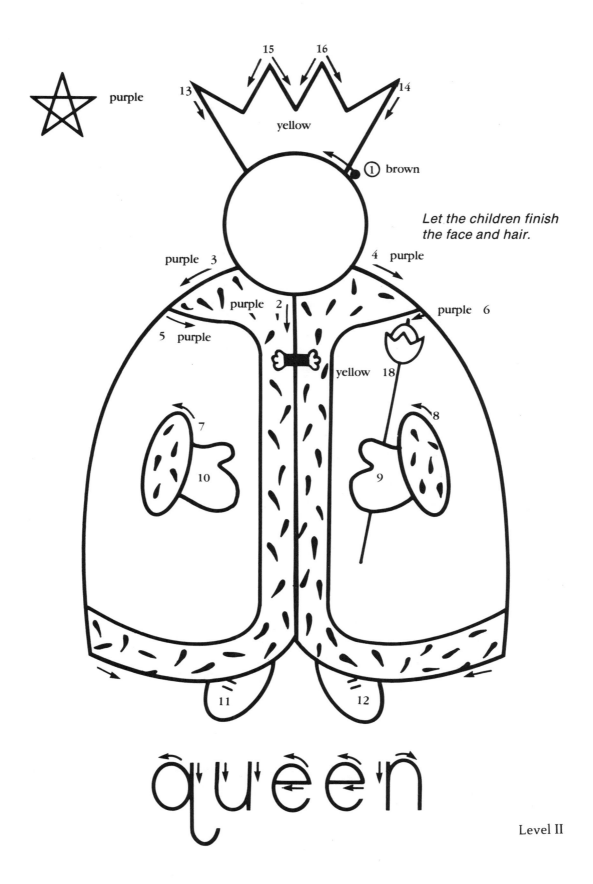

purple

15   16

13   14

yellow

① brown

Let the children finish
the face and hair.

purple 3   4 purple

purple 2

purple 6

5 purple

yellow 18

7   8

10   9

11   12

queen

Level II

SILLY SCRIBBLE TEACHER-DIRECTED PAGE

Level III

LETTER RECOGNITION: Q q
SILLY SCRIBBLE: quail
PAPER DIRECTION: "lying down"
STAR COLOR: blue

TEACHER DIRECTIONS: Look for the number 1. This will tell you where to make the START line and what color to use.

- Keep in mind the basic strokes described in Section 1.
- Always use the whole paper when doing Silly Scribbles.
- Always write the name of the Silly Scribble or encourage the children to try and write it themselves.
- Emphasize to the children that this is only one way of making a quail. Discuss other ways.

QUESTIONS YOU COULD ASK:

- Do you know what kind of bird this is?
- Have you ever seen a quail?
- Which line did you make first?
- What sound does "quail" begin with?

ADDITIONAL ACTIVITIES:

- Cut out eight different quails from construction paper (one out of each basic color). While the children cover their eyes, hide the quails somewhere in the room. Have the children go "quail hunting" and find the eight quails. Let them work in teams or give each different child a certain colored quail to find. Then let the children hide them again for others to find. Continue until every child has a chance to go "hunting."
- Share and discuss possibilities for these "qu" similes: "as quiet as a . . .," "as quick as a . . .," "as queasy as a . . .," etc.

CREATIVE THINKING STARTERS:

- Write a collaborative story about the "Quarreling Quail."

SUGGESTED READING:

- *A Is for Angry: An Animal & Adjective Alphabet* by Sandra Boynton. New York: Workman Publishing, 1983.

NOTES:

© 1989 by Shirley A. Steinmetz

Level III

quail

brown

brown

brown

brown

yellow and brown

orange

all brown

blue

orange

blue

SILLY SCRIBBLE TEACHER-DIRECTED PAGE

Level I

LETTER RECOGNITION: R r
SILLY SCRIBBLE: rabbit
PAPER DIRECTION: "standing up"
STAR COLOR: orange

TEACHER DIRECTIONS: Look for the number 1. This will tell you where to make the START line and what color to use.

- Keep in mind the basic strokes described in Section 1.
- Always use the whole paper when doing Silly Scribbles.
- Always write the name of the Silly Scribble or encourage the children to try and write it themselves.
- Emphasize to the children that this is only one way of making a rabbit. Discuss other ways.

QUESTIONS YOU COULD ASK:
- How many circles did we make?
- Which line did you make first? Last?

ADDITIONAL ACTIVITIES:
- Have a discussion about rabbits. Do a "web" with the children to find out what they already know about rabbits. (A web is like a flow chart.)
- Let the children paint or cut and paste a rabbit. Have the children tell or write about their picture. Make a rabbit-shaped book with a front cover as a face and the back cover as a tail.
- Can you hop like a rabbit? Count the hops it takes to get to the table, chair, etc.

CREATIVE THINKING STARTERS:
- Can you think of what a rabbit has that no other animal has?

SUGGESTED READING:
- *Huge Harold* by Bill Peet. Boston: Houghton Mifflin Company, 1961.
- *Let's Make Rabbits* by Leo Lionni. New York: Pantheon Books, 1982.
- *Home for a Bunny* by Margaret Wise Brown. Illustrated by Garth Williams. New York: Western Publishers, 1983.
- *The Country Bunny and the Little Gold Shoes* by Du Bose Heyward. Illustrated by Marjorie Flack. New York: Houghton Mifflin Company, 1939.

NOTES:

orange

all brown
①

8

7

10

2

3

12 green

4

11
orange

9

5

6

rabbit

Level I

SILLY SCRIBBLE TEACHER-DIRECTED PAGE

LETTER RECOGNITION: R r
SILLY SCRIBBLE: raccoon
PAPER DIRECTION: "standing up"
STAR COLOR: brown

TEACHER DIRECTIONS: Look for the number 1. This will tell you where to make the START line and what color to use.

- Keep in mind the basic strokes described in Section 1.
- Always use the whole paper when doing Silly Scribbles.
- Always write the name of the Silly Scribble or encourage the children to try and write it themselves.
- Emphasize to the children that this is only one way of making a raccoon. Discuss other ways.

QUESTIONS YOU COULD ASK:

- What was the first clue that it was a raccoon?
- What letter does "raccoon" begin with?
- How many whiskers did we make?
- When you write raccoon, discuss the letters that are doubled (cc, oo).

ADDITIONAL ACTIVITIES:

- Find out what a raccoon does with its food before it eats. Why?
- Make ten raccoons without tails. Number them 1 through 10. Make ten tails, with only the amount of stripes for that number. See if the children can match the striped tails to the correct raccoons.

CREATIVE THINKING STARTERS:

- Write two collaborative stories about "Robber Raccoon": one in which he is good and one in which he is not.

SUGGESTED READING:

- *Little Raccoon and the Thing in the Pond* by Lillian Moore. Illustrated by Gioia Flammenghi. New York: McGraw Hill, 1963.
- *Here Comes Raccoon!* by Lillian Hoban. New York: Holt, Rinehart and Winston, 1977.

NOTES:

 brown

① all brown with black

red berry

raccoon

Level II

SILLY SCRIBBLE TEACHER-DIRECTED PAGE

Level III

LETTER RECOGNITION: R r
SILLY SCRIBBLE: rhinoceros (black)
PAPER DIRECTION: "lying down"
STAR COLOR: black

TEACHER DIRECTIONS: Look for the number 1. This will tell you where to make the START line and what color to use.

- Keep in mind the basic strokes described in Section 1.
- Always use the whole paper when doing Silly Scribbles.
- Always write the name of the Silly Scribble or encourage the children to try and write it themselves.
- Emphasize to the children that this is only one way of making a rhinoceros. Discuss other ways.

QUESTIONS YOU COULD ASK:

- What was your first clue to what this Silly Scribble was?
- What sound does "rhinoceros" begin with?
- Can you think of another animal that has feet like this?
- Did you know that of the five different kinds of rhinoceros, most are very rare and protected by laws?

ADDITIONAL ACTIVITIES:

- Make a cardboard head of a rhinoceros with the two horns. Let the children throw rings around them.
- Discuss why a rhinoceros seems so grumpy. Let the children draw pictures and write or tell their reason. Make a book called "Why the Rhino Is So Grumpy!"

CREATIVE THINKING STARTERS:

- Would you like a rhinoceros for a pet? Why?

SUGGESTED READING:

- *Who Wants a Cheap Rhinoceros?* by Shel Silverstein. New York: Macmillan, 1964.

NOTES:

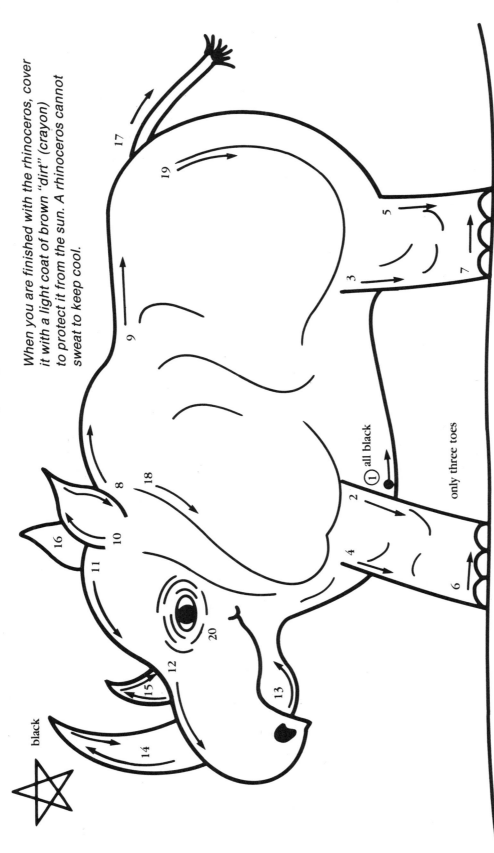

When you are finished with the rhinoceros, cover it with a light coat of brown "dirt" (crayon) to protect it from the sun. A rhinoceros cannot sweat to keep cool.

all black

only three toes

black

Level III

rhinoceros

SILLY SCRIBBLE TEACHER-DIRECTED PAGE

Level I

LETTER RECOGNITION: S s
SILLY SCRIBBLE: stoplight
PAPER DIRECTION: "standing up"
STAR COLOR: green

TEACHER DIRECTIONS: Look for the number 1. This will tell you where to make the START line and what color to use.

- Keep in mind the basic strokes described in Section 1.
- Always use the whole paper when doing Silly Scribbles.
- Always write the name of the Silly Scribble or encourage the children to try and write it themselves.
- Emphasize to the children that this is only one way of making a stoplight. Discuss other ways.

QUESTIONS YOU COULD ASK:

- Which color is at the top? Middle? Bottom?
- What shapes did we use to make the stoplight?
- Did you know that the stoplight was invented in 1923 by a black American inventor named Garrett Augustus Morgan?

ADDITIONAL ACTIVITIES:

- Discuss safety and what the lights on the stoplight mean.
- Make a large stoplight with cellophane paper circles in the correct colors. Using a flashlight to show which one is "on," have a child be the stoplight and shine the flashlight behind the correct circle. Let the children do different movement activities and when the light is behind the red, they stop. (Behind green, they can move again; behind yellow, they have to move in slow motion.)

CREATIVE THINKING STARTERS:

- Why do you think Mr. Morgan came up with the idea for the stoplight? Why do you think they used the color red for stop? Yellow for caution? Green for go? Why not blue for stop?

SUGGESTED READING:

- *I Read Symbols* by Tana Hoban. New York: Greenwillow Books, 1983.

NOTES:

 green

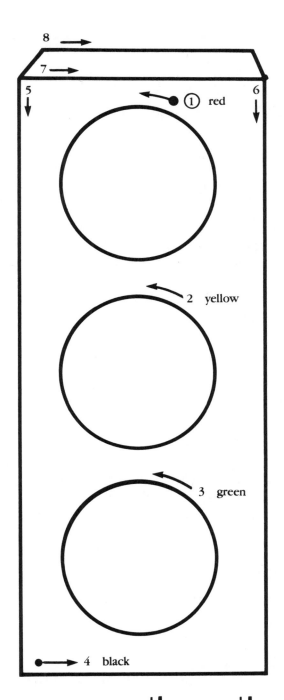

8 →

7 →

5 ↓   ← • ① red   6 ↓

← 2 yellow

← 3 green

• → 4 black

stoplight

Level I

SILLY SCRIBBLE TEACHER-DIRECTED PAGE

Level II

LETTER RECOGNITION: S s
SILLY SCRIBBLE: scarecrow
PAPER DIRECTION: "standing up"
STAR COLOR: orange

TEACHER DIRECTIONS: Look for the number 1. This will tell you where to make the START line and what color to use.

- Keep in mind the basic strokes described in Section 1.
- Always use the whole paper when doing Silly Scribbles.
- Always write the name of the Silly Scribble or encourage the children to try and write it themselves.
- Emphasize to the children that this is only one way of making a scarecrow. Discuss other ways.

QUESTIONS YOU COULD ASK:

- What was your first clue to what this Silly Scribble was?
- Why does the scarecrow have patches?
- What does a farmer put inside a scarecrow? What other things could be used?
- What is a scarecrow supposed to do?

ADDITIONAL ACTIVITIES:

- Pretend you are a scarecrow hanging on a post. I'm taking you down, so what will you do? How will you walk? What will your arms be like?
- Play "Simon Says" while the children pretend to be scarecrows.
- Have a "Scarecrow Day" and let the children dress like scarecrows. Be sure to bring in a selection of old hats, bandannas, shirts, and gloves for children who don't have "scarecrow" clothes.

CREATIVE THINKING STARTERS:

- Write a collaborative story about "The First Scarecrow."

SUGGESTED READING:

- *Sam the Scarecrow* by Sharon Gordon. Illustrated by Don Silverstein. Mahwah, NJ: Troll Associates, 1980.
- *The Wizard of Oz* by Frank L. Baum. Illustrated by Evelyn Copelman. New York: Putnam, 1956.

NOTES:

orange

18

16
17
19

1

brown
21

20

22 black
23 black

2
3
4

7
9
10 6
8

5

all
straw is brown
and yellow

© 1989 by Shirley A. Steinmetz

11

12
13

24
black

14
15

scarecrow

Level II

SILLY SCRIBBLE TEACHER-DIRECTED PAGE

LETTER RECOGNITION: S s
SILLY SCRIBBLE: skunk
PAPER DIRECTION: "lying down"
STAR COLOR: black

TEACHER DIRECTIONS: Look for the number 1. This will tell you where to make the START line and what color to use.

- Keep in mind the basic strokes described in Section 1.
- Always use the whole paper when doing Silly Scribbles.
- Always write the name of the Silly Scribble or encourage the children to try and write it themselves.
- Emphasize to the children that this is only one way of making a skunk. Discuss other ways.

QUESTIONS YOU COULD ASK:

- What was your first clue to what this Silly Scribble was?
- Have you ever seen a skunk?
- What was the first line we made?
- If a skunk stamps its feet at you, growls, or lifts its tail, what do you think it is getting ready to do? (Spray!)

ADDITIONAL ACTIVITIES:

- Discuss smell as one of the five senses.
- Make a book of good and bad smells suggested by the children.
- Put lemon, garlic, onion, peppermint, almond extract, licorice, floor wax, coffee, and soap into different containers and cover with lids. Punch holes and let the children guess what they smell.
- Discuss blends and digraphs: sk, bl, gr, st, sh, th.

CREATIVE THINKING STARTERS:

- Have you ever smelled a skunk? When?

SUGGESTED READING:

- *The Littlest Skunk* by Theresa Kalab Smith. Austin, TX: Steck-Vaughn Company, 1964.

NOTES:

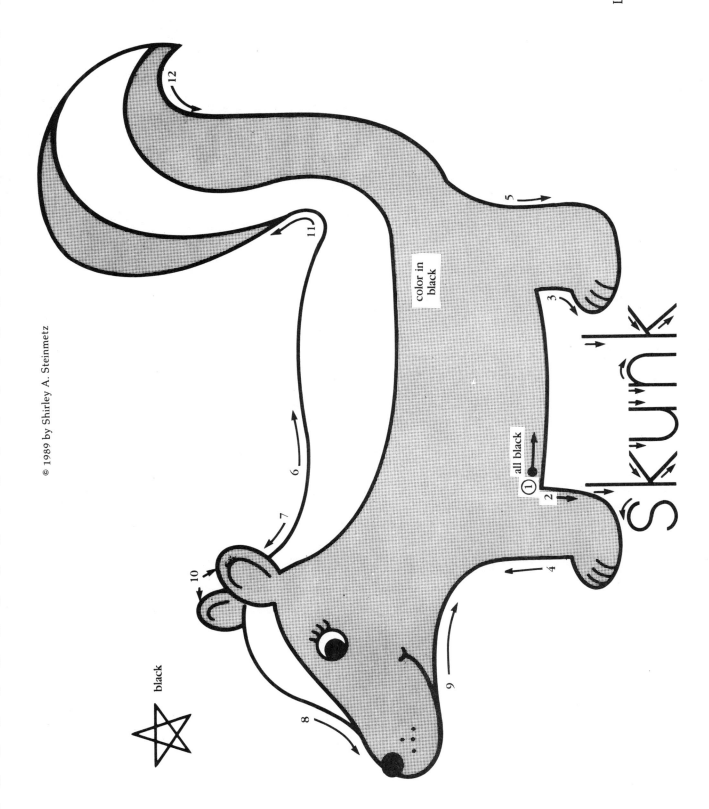

Level III

© 1989 by Shirley A. Steinmetz

color in black

all black

Skunk

black

SILLY SCRIBBLE TEACHER-DIRECTED PAGE

Level I

LETTER RECOGNITION: T t
SILLY SCRIBBLE: trout (rainbow)
PAPER DIRECTION: "lying down"
STAR COLOR: blue

TEACHER DIRECTIONS: Look for the number 1. This will tell you where to make the START line and what color to use.

- Keep in mind the basic strokes described in Section 1.
- Always use the whole paper when doing Silly Scribbles.
- Always write the name of the Silly Scribble or encourage the children to try and write it themselves.
- Emphasize to the children that this is only one way of making a rainbow trout. Discuss other ways.

QUESTIONS YOU COULD ASK:

- What was your first clue to what this Silly Scribble was?
- Have you ever seen a rainbow trout?
- Have you ever eaten one?
- What sound does "trout" begin with?
- Did you know that the rainbow trout is one of the most fun fish to catch because they fight so hard when caught on a line?

ADDITIONAL ACTIVITIES:

- Discuss how to make a rainbow.
- Let the children paint rainbow pictures.
- Bring in a small rainbow trout for the children to examine in a fishbowl.
- Serve fish sticks for a snack.
- Discuss "scales" on a fish.
- Bring in a fishing pole and let the children practice "casting" for fish outside on a cement area. Have some parents come in with their poles to show the children how. Be sure to set up safety rules.

CREATIVE THINKING STARTERS:

- Can you think of any other animal, fish, or bird that has a rainbow?

SUGGESTED READING:

- *Trout the Magnificent* by Sheila Turnage. Illustrated by Janet Stevens. New York: Harcourt, Brace, Jovanovich, 1984.
- *Roses are Red. Are Violets Blue?* by Alice and Martin Provensen. New York: Random House, 1973.

NOTES:

When you are finished, let the children put rainbow stripes on the trout to color it in.

① all black

8

7

14

17

16

6

15

13

12

18

11

10

9

19 orange

3

2

4

5

blue

blue smile lines

trout

SILLY SCRIBBLE TEACHER-DIRECTED PAGE

Level II

LETTER RECOGNITION: T t
SILLY SCRIBBLE: turkey
PAPER DIRECTION: "lying down"
STAR COLOR: orange

TEACHER DIRECTIONS: Look for the number 1. This will tell you where to make the START line and what color to use.

- Keep in mind the basic strokes described in Section 1.
- Always use the whole paper when doing Silly Scribbles.
- Always write the name of the Silly Scribble or encourage the children to try and write it themselves.
- Emphasize to the children that this is only one way to make a turkey. Discuss other ways.

QUESTIONS YOU COULD ASK:
- What shape is the body?
- How many tail feathers does the turkey have?
- What sound does "turkey" begin with?
- Have you ever eaten turkey meat?
- What sound does a turkey make?

ADDITIONAL ACTIVITIES:
- Make a large turkey with no tail. Make and number ten feathers for the tail, and let the children put on the feathers starting on the left and going around to the right in numerical order.
- Make a graph of the children who like light, dark, no turkey meat, or are vegetarians and don't eat meat at all.

CREATIVE THINKING STARTERS:
- What is the red thing on the turkey's beak called? What do you think it is used for? (Snood or dewbill is on top of the beak and the wattle is under the beak on the throat.)

SUGGESTED READING:
- *One Tough Turkey* by Steven Kroll. Illustrated by John Wagner. New York: Holiday House, 1982.

NOTES:

orange

7

8

9

all brown

orange   red

4

2   3

5   6

10

11

12   13

14

turkey

Level II

SILLY SCRIBBLE TEACHER-DIRECTED PAGE

LETTER RECOGNITION: T t
SILLY SCRIBBLE: tyrannosaurus rex
PAPER DIRECTION: "standing up"
STAR COLOR: brown

TEACHER DIRECTIONS: Look for the number 1. This will tell you where to make the START line and what color to use.

- Keep in mind the basic strokes described in Section 1.
- Always use the whole paper when doing Silly Scribbles.
- Always write the name of the Silly Scribble or encourage the children to try and write it themselves.
- Emphasize to the children that this is only one way to make a tyrannosaurus rex. Discuss other ways.

QUESTIONS YOU COULD ASK:

- What was your first clue to what this Silly Scribble was?
- Do you know which dinosaur this is?
- Do you think this dinosaur ate meat or plants? How can you tell?

ADDITIONAL ACTIVITIES:

- Discuss dinosaurs and make a list of what the children know. How many different dinosaurs can they name?
- After reading, watching videos or movies and looking at pictures, discuss and compare the difference between the time when dinosaurs were on earth to what it is like now.
- Discuss "extinct."

CREATIVE THINKING STARTERS:

- If dinosaurs were alive today, do you think they would be tame? What uses could a dinosaur have today?

SUGGESTED READING:

- *Patrick's Dinosaur* by Carol Carrick. Illustrated by Donald Carrick. New York: Clarion Books/Ticknor and Fields, 1983.
- *Danny and the Dinosaur* by Syd Hoff. New York: Harper & Row, 1958.
- *Prehistoric Monsters Did the Strangest Things* by Leonora and Arthur Hornblow. Illustrated by Michael K. Firth. New York: Random House, 1974.

NOTES:

① all brown

2

3

4

5

6

7

8

9

10

11

12

13

14

15

tyrannosaurus
rex

Level II

SILLY SCRIBBLE TEACHER-DIRECTED PAGE

LETTER RECOGNITION: U u
SILLY SCRIBBLE: umbrella
PAPER DIRECTION: "lying down"
STAR COLOR: blue

TEACHER DIRECTIONS: Look for the number 1. This will tell you where to make the START line and what color to use.

- Keep in mind the basic strokes described in Section 1.
- Always use the whole paper when doing Silly Scribbles.
- Always write the name of the Silly Scribble or encourage the children to try and write it themselves.
- Emphasize to the children that this is only one way of making an umbrella. Discuss other ways.

QUESTIONS YOU COULD ASK:

- What was your first clue to what this Silly Scribble was?
- Do you know what sound "umbrella" begins with?
- How many hearts did we make?

ADDITIONAL ACTIVITIES:

- On a rainy day, have the children bring in their umbrellas. Compare and sort them into different categories.
- Examine an umbrella together. Note how the ribs work and what makes it open and shut.
- Share the saying, "April Showers Bring May Flowers." Discuss why this might be so.

CREATIVE THINKING STARTERS:

- Why do you think some people think it is bad luck to open an umbrella inside a building? Discuss superstitions.

SUGGESTED READING:

- *Umbrella* by Taro Yashima. New York: Viking Press, 1958.
- *Take Another Look* by Tana Hoban. New York: Greenwillow Books, 1981.

NOTES:

8

red hearts

6

5

7

4

3

2

purple ①

blue

umbrella

SILLY SCRIBBLE TEACHER-DIRECTED PAGE

LETTER RECOGNITION: U u
SILLY SCRIBBLE: upside down
PAPER DIRECTION: "standing up"
STAR COLOR: blue

TEACHER DIRECTIONS: Look for the number 1. This will tell you where to make the START line and what color to use.

- Keep in mind the basic strokes described in Section 1.
- Always use the whole paper when doing Silly Scribbles.
- Always write the name of the Silly Scribble or encourage the children to try and write it themselves.
- Emphasize to the children that this is only one way of making an opossum. Discuss other ways.

QUESTIONS YOU COULD ASK:

- What do you think is hanging on the branch?
- Do you know what sound this animal's name begins with? This animal is also sometimes called a "possum." What sound does "possum" begin with?
- Do you remember the last line we made?

ADDITIONAL ACTIVITIES:

- Have the children draw a picture of themselves upside down.
- Using letter cards, see if the children can tell what the letter is if you hold it upside down.
- Discuss how the opossum fools animals who want to eat it.

CREATIVE THINKING STARTERS:

- Can you think of any other animals that might hang upside down?

SUGGESTED READING:

- *Inside, Outside, Upside Down* by Stan and Jan Berenstain. New York: Random House, 1968.
- *Henry Possum* by Harold Berson. New York: Crown Publishers, 1973.
- *Burton and Dudley* by Marjorie Weinman Sharmat. Illustrated by Barbara Cooney. New York: Holiday House, 1975.
- *Possum* by Robert M. McClung. New York: William Morrow and Company, 1963.

NOTES:

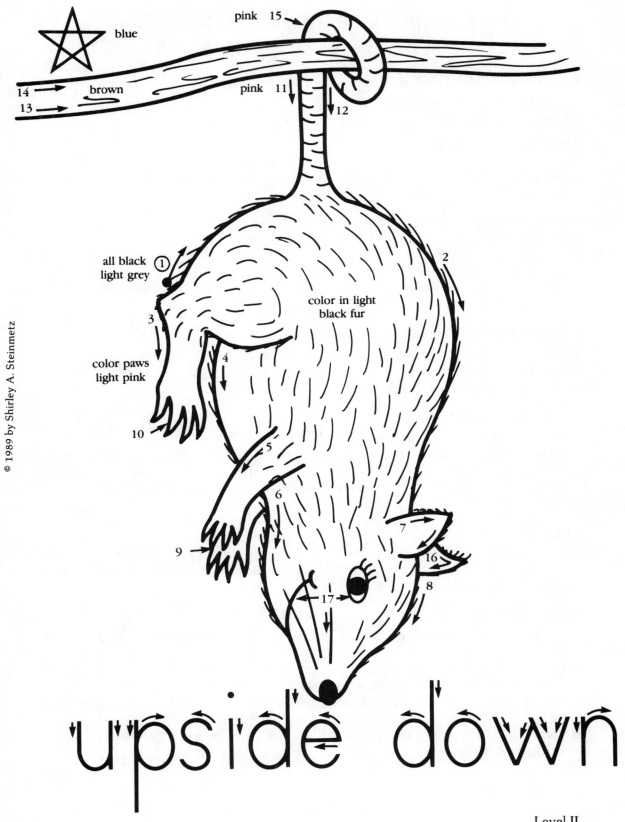

blue

pink 15

pink 11

12

14 brown

13

all black
light grey ①

color in light
black fur

2

3

color paws
light pink

4

10

5

6

7

9

16

8

17

upside down

Level II

SILLY SCRIBBLE TEACHER-DIRECTED PAGE

LETTER RECOGNITION: U u
SILLY SCRIBBLE: unicorn
PAPER DIRECTION: "lying down"
STAR COLOR: blue

TEACHER DIRECTIONS: Look for the number 1. This will tell you where to make the START line and what color to use.

- Keep in mind the basic strokes described in Section 1.
- Always use the whole paper when doing Silly Scribbles.
- Always write the name of the Silly Scribble or encourage the children to try and write it themselves.
- Emphasize to the children that this is only one way of making a unicorn. Discuss other ways.

QUESTIONS YOU COULD ASK:

- What was your first clue to what this Silly Scribble was?
- Do you know what sound "unicorn" begins with?
- Do you remember which line we made first? Second?

ADDITIONAL ACTIVITIES:

- Discuss unicorns and list what the children know about them.
- After reading and looking at pictures of unicorns, with the children make a list of descriptive words that could be used to describe a unicorn. (For example, enchanted, wistful, joyful, kind, wondrous, unusual, unique, beautiful.)
- Discuss vowels.

CREATIVE THINKING STARTERS:

- Do you believe in unicorns? Why or why not? A long, long time ago most people believed in unicorns. Why do you think most people do not believe in unicorns today?

SUGGESTED READING:

- *The Unicorn and the Lake* by Marianna Mayer. Illustrated by Michael Hague. New York: Dial Press, 1982.
- *If I Found a Wistful Unicorn* by Ann Ashford. Illustrated by Bill Drath. Atlanta: Peachtree Publishers, Ltd., 1978.
- *Sarah's Unicorn* by Bruce and Katherine Coville. New York: J. B. Lippincott, 1979.
- *Unicorn and the Plow* by Louise Moeri. Illustrated by Diane Goode. New York: E. P. Dutton, 1982.

NOTES:

© 1989 by Shirley A. Steinmetz

all black

brown eye

15 yellow

blue

green grass

Level III

unicorn

SILLY SCRIBBLE TEACHER-DIRECTED PAGE

Level I

LETTER RECOGNITION: V v
SILLY SCRIBBLE: valentine
PAPER DIRECTION: "standing up"
STAR COLOR: red

TEACHER DIRECTIONS: Look for the number 1. This will tell you where to make the START line and what color to use.

- Keep in mind the basic strokes described in Section 1.
- Always use the whole paper when doing Silly Scribbles.
- Always write the name of the Silly Scribble or encourage the children to try and write it themselves.
- Emphasize to the children that this is only one way of making a valentine. Discuss other ways.

QUESTIONS YOU COULD ASK:

- Do you know what this valentine says?
- Do you know what sound "valentine" begins with?

ADDITIONAL ACTIVITIES:

- Have the children make a valentine for someone, even if it isn't Valentine's Day.
- Show the children how to cut valentines on the fold and let them practice on scrap paper.
- Have the children make a book about people they love.
- Start a post office and let the children send letters or pictures to each other.

CREATIVE THINKING STARTERS:

- Who is the most important person in the world? You are! Share something that you like about yourself.

SUGGESTED READING:

- *One Zillion Valentines* by Frank Modell. New York: Greenwillow Books, 1981.
- *Our Valentine Book* by Jane Belk Moncure. Illustrated by Mina Gow McLean. Chicago: Children's Press, 1976.

NOTES:

red

© 1989 by Shirley A. Steinmetz

9

8

6

7

2

4

3

5

I Love
You

10

① all
red

valentine

Level I

SILLY SCRIBBLE TEACHER-DIRECTED PAGE

LETTER RECOGNITION: V v
SILLY SCRIBBLE: vegetables
PAPER DIRECTION: "lying down"
STAR COLOR: orange

TEACHER DIRECTIONS: Look for the number 1. This will tell you where to make the START line and what color to use.

- Keep in mind the basic strokes described in Section 1.
- Always use the whole paper when doing Silly Scribbles.
- Always write the name of the Silly Scribble or encourage the children to try and write it themselves.
- Emphasize to the children that this is only one way of making these vegetables. Discuss other ways.

QUESTIONS YOU COULD ASK:

- What was the first clue you had that these Silly Scribbles were vegetables?
- Which one of these is your favorite?
- What was the first vegetable we made? Second? Third?

ADDITIONAL ACTIVITIES:

- Make vegetable prints.
- Enjoy vegetables and a dip for snack.
- Make a graph of the children's favorite vegetable.
- Make a list of all the vegetables the children know.
- Discuss what happens to vegetables when they are cooked. How do they change? Bring in some vegetables and eat some raw. Then cook them. You may want to let the children predict what will happen. Compare the cooked vegetables to the raw vegetables and discuss how they changed.

CREATIVE THINKING STARTERS:

- Can you create a new vegetable? A green carrot? A bumpy tomato?

SUGGESTED READING:

- *The Giant Vegetable Garden* by Nadine Bernard Westcott. Boston: Little, Brown and Company, 1981.
- *Stone Soup* by Marcia Brown. New York: Charles Scribner and Sons, 1947.

NOTES:

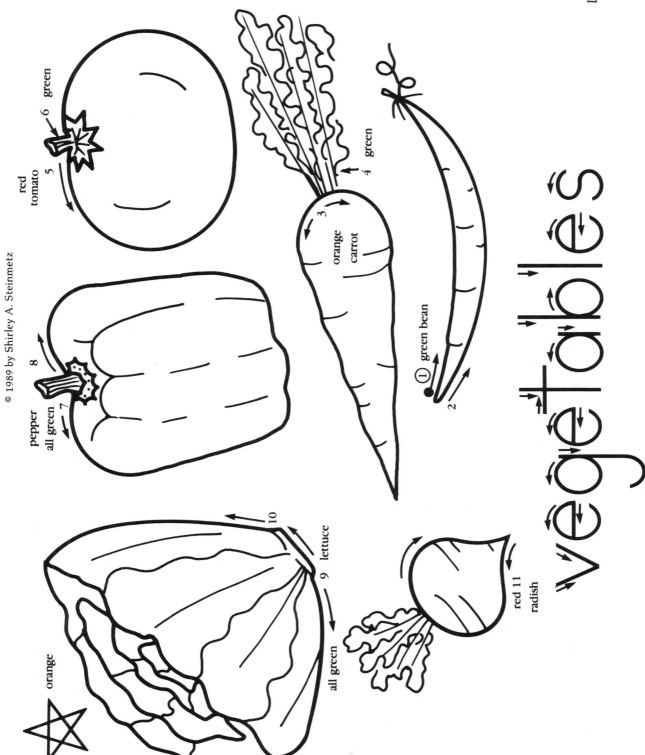

vegetables

red
tomato
green

pepper
all green

orange
carrot
green

① green bean

orange

lettuce
all green

red
radish

SILLY SCRIBBLE TEACHER-DIRECTED PAGE

Level III

LETTER RECOGNITION: V v
SILLY SCRIBBLE: vulture
PAPER DIRECTION: "standing up"
STAR COLOR: black

TEACHER DIRECTIONS: Look for the number 1. This will tell you where to make the START line and what color to use.

- Keep in mind the basic strokes described in Section 1.
- Always use the whole paper when doing Silly Scribbles.
- Always write the name of the Silly Scribble or encourage the children to try and write it themselves.
- Emphasize to the children that this is only one way of making a vulture. Discuss other ways.

QUESTIONS YOU COULD ASK:
- What kind of bird is this?
- Do you know what sound "vulture" begins with?
- Looking at this Silly Scribble, does Stan or Carla make the most lines?
- Did you know that a vulture will throw up if scared or caught?

ADDITIONAL ACTIVITIES:
- Discuss and make a list of what the children know about vultures.
- Explore birds and what they eat. Compare and classify them.
- Make a large vulture. Tell a story about the many different things it eats. Have pictures of many silly things, such as a piano, car, cake. See if the children can remember the sequence and then feed the vulture. If you do this more than once, change the sequence to see if the children can remember.

CREATIVE THINKING STARTERS:
- Would you like a vulture for a pet? Why?

SUGGESTED READING:
- *Eli* by Bill Peet. Boston: Houghton Mifflin Company, 1987.

NOTES:

black

black

orange 10

9

red ①   2

11

black

12   5   black

color
black

4   black

black 3

leave
white

6 black

orange 7   orange 8

© 1989 by Shirley A. Steinmetz

vulture

Level III

SILLY SCRIBBLE TEACHER-DIRECTED PAGE

Level I

LETTER RECOGNITION: W w
SILLY SCRIBBLE: windmill
PAPER DIRECTION: "standing up"
STAR COLOR: red

TEACHER DIRECTIONS: Look for the number 1. This will tell you where to make the START line and what color to use.

- Keep in mind the basic strokes described in Section 1.
- Always use the whole paper when doing Silly Scribbles.
- Always write the name of the Silly Scribble or encourage the children to try and write it themselves.
- Emphasize to the children that this is only one way of making a windmill. Discuss other ways.

QUESTIONS YOU COULD ASK:

- What was your first clue to what this Silly Scribble was?
- How many ovals do you see?
- How many flowers did we make altogether?
- What makes the windmill go around?
- What sound does "windmill" begin with?
- Which lines are Stan "slide" lines?

ADDITIONAL ACTIVITIES:

- Help the children make pinwheels to take outside.
- Discuss wind and how it helps us. Power? Seeds? Sailboats? Kites?
- Plant some tulip bulbs in the fall and see what happens in the spring. (Or force start some bulbs in water and charcoal.)
- Discuss compound words.

CREATIVE THINKING STARTERS:

- Find out why the Dutch built the windmill in Holland and what it does even today.

SUGGESTED READING:

- *The Wind Blew* by Pat Hutchins. New York: Macmillan Publishing Company, 1974.
- *The Hole in the Dike*, retold by Norma Green. Illustrated by Eric Carle. New York: Thomas Y. Crowell Company, 1974. (This is an adaptation of *Hans Brinker, or The Silver Skates* by Mary Mapes Dodge.)

NOTES:

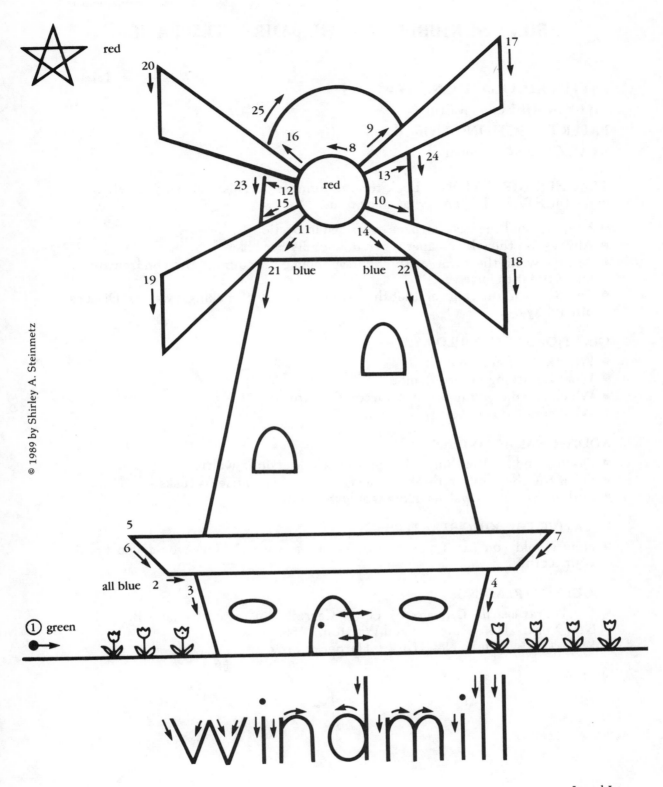

red

© 1989 by Shirley A. Steinmetz

red

all blue

blue   blue

① green

Level I

SILLY SCRIBBLE TEACHER-DIRECTED PAGE

LETTER RECOGNITION: W w
SILLY SCRIBBLE: walrus
PAPER DIRECTION: "lying down"
STAR COLOR: brown

TEACHER DIRECTIONS: Look for the number 1. This will tell you where to make the START line and what color to use.

- Keep in mind the basic strokes described in Section 1.
- Always use the whole paper when doing Silly Scribbles.
- Always write the name of the Silly Scribble or encourage the children to try and write it themselves.
- Emphasize to the children that this is only one way of making a walrus. Discuss other ways.

QUESTIONS YOU COULD ASK:
- What kind of animal is this?
- What is sticking out of its mouth?
- Which line did you make first? Second? Third?
- What sound does "walrus" end with?

ADDITIONAL ACTIVITIES:
- Discuss and list the things the children know about a walrus.
- See if the children can think of ways a walrus would use its tusks.
- Pretend you are a walrus. How would you move?

CREATIVE THINKING STARTERS:
- How would you eat if you had tusks like a walrus? How would you brush your teeth?

SUGGESTED READING:
- *The Walrus and the Carpenter* by Lewis Carroll. Illustrated by Jane B. Zalben. New York: Holt, Rinehart and Winston, 1986.
- *Walspot* by Syd Hoff. New York: Harper & Row, 1977.

NOTES:

Level II

walrus

all brown ①

brown

2

3

4

5

6

7

8

9

10

SILLY SCRIBBLE TEACHER-DIRECTED PAGE

Level III

LETTER RECOGNITION: W w
SILLY SCRIBBLE: woodpecker
PAPER DIRECTION: "standing up"
STAR COLOR: black

TEACHER DIRECTIONS: Look for the number 1. This will tell you where to make the START line and what color to use.

- Keep in mind the basic strokes described in Section 1.
- Always use the whole paper when doing Silly Scribbles.
- Always write the name of the Silly Scribble or encourage the children to try and write it themselves.
- Emphasize to the children that this is only one way of making a woodpecker. Discuss other ways.

QUESTIONS YOU COULD ASK:
- What kind of bird is this?
- How do you think it hangs onto the tree?
- What is in the hole that the woodpecker wants?
- Have you ever heard a woodpecker?

ADDITIONAL ACTIVITIES:
- Set up a building center and let the children create with wood, nails, and so forth. Be sure you closely supervise the children!
- Make a bird book.

CREATIVE THINKING STARTERS:
- Why do you think the woodpecker doesn't break its beak? What would happen if it did?

SUGGESTED READING:
- Bring in some *Woody Woodpecker* comic books and discuss them: how they are put together and the sequence of pictures. You might want to cut some apart and let the children put them back in order.

NOTES:

black

① brown tree

2

10

red

3

red

color in
black

4

9

5

11
orange

red

6

7

8

© 1989 by Shirley A. Steinmetz

woodpecker

Level III

SILLY SCRIBBLE TEACHER-DIRECTED PAGE

LETTER RECOGNITION: X x
SILLY SCRIBBLE: railroad crossing sign
PAPER DIRECTION: "standing up"
STAR COLOR: black

TEACHER DIRECTIONS: Look for the number 1. This will tell you where to make the START line and what color to use.

- Keep in mind the basic strokes described in Section 1.
- Always use the whole paper when doing Silly Scribbles.
- Always write the name of the Silly Scribble or encourage the children to try and write it themselves.
- Emphasize to the children that this is only one way of making a railroad crossing sign. Discuss other ways.

QUESTIONS YOU COULD ASK:

- Do you know what sign this is?
- What does this sign tell you?
- What is the letter in the middle of this sign?

ADDITIONAL ACTIVITIES:

- Discuss trains. If you have a small set, display it in the room.
- Pretend the children are a train. Discuss the engine, caboose, and so forth. Then "ch-oo-oo-oo" around the room.
- Discuss the many different kinds of signs in the world and what they mean. With the children, make a collection of different kinds of signs, such as labels, bumper stickers, trademarks, and logos.

CREATIVE THINKING STARTERS:

- What other "crossing" signs have you seen? Can you make up your own? Worm crossing? Penguin crossing?

SUGGESTED READING:

- *I Read Symbols* by Tana Hoban. New York: Greenwillow Books, 1983.
- *Freight Train* by Donald Crews. New York: Greenwillow Books, 1978.

NOTES:

black

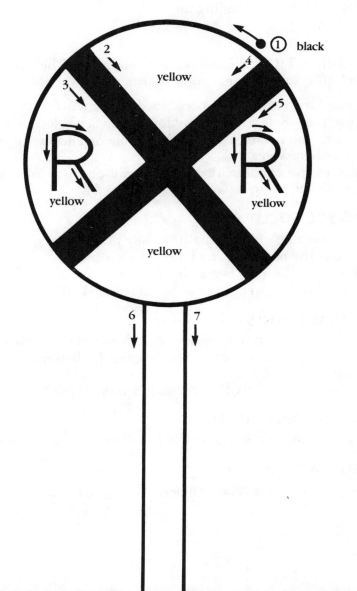

① black

2

yellow

3   4

5

R   R

yellow   yellow

yellow

6   7

8 → green

railroad

Level I

SILLY SCRIBBLE TEACHER-DIRECTED PAGE

LETTER RECOGNITION: X x   **Level II**

SILLY SCRIBBLE: X-ray

PAPER DIRECTION: "standing up"

STAR COLOR: black

TEACHER DIRECTIONS: Look for the number 1. This will tell you where to make the START line and what color to use.

- Keep in mind the basic strokes described in Section 1.
- Always use the whole paper when doing Silly Scribbles.
- Always write the name of the Silly Scribble or encourage the children to try and write it themselves.
- Emphasize to the children that this is only one way of making an X-ray of a skeleton. Discuss other ways.

QUESTIONS YOU COULD ASK:

- What was your first clue to what this Silly Scribble was?
- Do you know the names of any bones in your body?
- What sound does "X-ray" begin with?
- Do you know which part of the skeleton is the skull?

ADDITIONAL ACTIVITIES:

- Borrow a skeleton from the high school, if possible, and discuss the bones.
- Look at skeleton pictures of different animals, fish, and/or birds. See if the children can tell what it is.
- Play body-awareness activities, such as "Simon Says."

CREATIVE THINKING STARTERS:

- How do you think you would look if you did not have a skeleton?

SUGGESTED READING:

- *Funnybones* by Janet and Allan Ahlberg. New York: Scholastic Book Services, 1980.

NOTES:

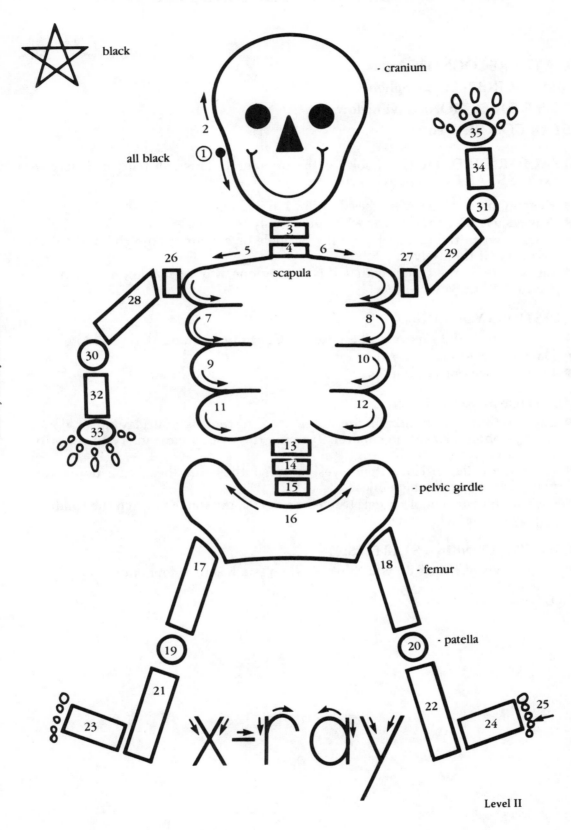

black

- cranium

all black

scapula

- pelvic girdle

- femur

- patella

x-ray

Level II

© 1989 by Shirley A. Steinmetz

SILLY SCRIBBLE TEACHER-DIRECTED PAGE

Level III
Go slow, very difficult

LETTER RECOGNITION: X x
SILLY SCRIBBLE: xylophone
PAPER DIRECTION: "lying down"
STAR COLOR: red

TEACHER DIRECTIONS: Look for the number 1. This will tell you where to make the START line and what color to use.

- Keep in mind the basic strokes described in Section 1.
- Always use the whole paper when doing Silly Scribbles.
- Always write the name of the Silly Scribble or encourage the children to try and write it themselves.
- Emphasize to the children that this is only one way of making a xylophone. Discuss other ways.

QUESTIONS YOU COULD ASK:
- What color is the bar with "C1"? "G5"? (Continue, naming all the bars.)
- Have you ever played a xylophone?
- Do you have one at home?

ADDITIONAL ACTIVITIES:
- Discuss that the sounds of the notes are different as you play up or down the xylophone. Have the children examine the xylophone and try to see why this is so.
- Have the children close their eyes to see if they can "hear" the notes you play. Can they tell which ones?
- Visit with your school's music teacher and get some songs to teach the children to play on the xylophone.

CREATIVE THINKING STARTERS:
- What kinds of things do you think of when you hear a xylophone?

NOTES:

xylophone

Level III

© 1989 by Shirley A. Steinmetz

	red	orange	yellow	green	blue	black	white	purple
	C	D	E	F	G	A	B	C
	1	2	3	4	5	6	7	8

① red

red 3
4
5 7
8
9 11
12
13 15
16
17 19
20
21 23
24
25 27
28
29 31
32

2 red
6
10
14
18
22
26
30

33 black
34 black

36 black
35 black

SILLY SCRIBBLE TEACHER-DIRECTED PAGE

Level I

LETTER RECOGNITION: Y y
SILLY SCRIBBLE: yo-yo
PAPER DIRECTION: "standing up"
STAR COLOR: blue

TEACHER DIRECTIONS: Look for the number 1. This will tell you where to make the START line and what color to use.

- Keep in mind the basic strokes described in Section 1.
- Always use the whole paper when doing Silly Scribbles.
- Always write the name of the Silly Scribble or encourage the children to try and write it themselves.
- Emphasize to the children that this is only one way of making a yo-yo. Discuss other ways.

QUESTIONS YOU COULD ASK:
- What shape is this?
- What is the string for?
- What is the name of this toy?

ADDITIONAL ACTIVITIES:
- Have fun with a yo-yo. Bring in some for the children to try.
- Discuss the different things you can make a yo-yo do.
- See if someone can come in and show your class some yo-yo tricks. Maybe an older student? A parent?

CREATIVE THINKING STARTERS:
- What other games can you think of or invent using a string?

SUGGESTED READING:
- *When Panda Came to Our House* by Helen Jane Jensen. New York: Dial Books for Young Readers, 1985.

NOTES:

 blue

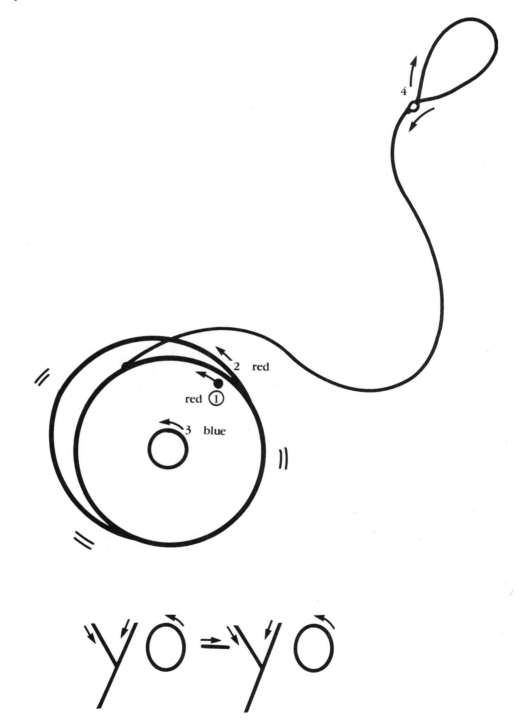

Level I

SILLY SCRIBBLE TEACHER-DIRECTED PAGE

Level II

LETTER RECOGNITION: Y y
SILLY SCRIBBLE: yucky
PAPER DIRECTION: "lying down"
STAR COLOR: green

TEACHER DIRECTIONS: Look for the number 1. This will tell you where to make the START line and what color to use.

- Keep in mind the basic strokes described in Section 1.
- Always use the whole paper when doing Silly Scribbles.
- Always write the name of the Silly Scribble or encourage the children to try and write it themselves.
- Emphasize to the children that this is only one way of making something yucky. Discuss other ways.

QUESTIONS YOU COULD ASK:

- What do you think this is?
- Would you want to eat it?
- What sound does "yucky" begin with?

ADDITIONAL ACTIVITIES:

- Have the children make a list of yucky things.
- Make yucky faces. Bring in a mirror and let the children watch themselves as they make yucky faces.
- Make a list of foods that the children think are yucky.
- Look through food and fashion magazines and collect some yucky pictures.

CREATIVE THINKING STARTERS:

- What is the "yuckiest" thing you can think of? Draw a picture.

SUGGESTED READING:

- *More Spaghetti, I Say!* by Golden Gelman. Illustrated by Jack Kent. New York: Scholastic, 1977.
- *Bartholomew and the Oobleck* by Dr. Seuss. New York: Random House, 1949.
- *Harry and the Terrible Whatzit* by Dick Gackenbach. New York: Scholastic Book Services, 1977.

NOTES:

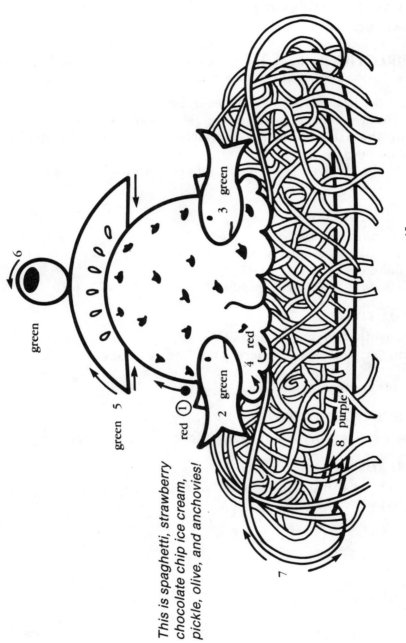

This is spaghetti, strawberry chocolate chip ice cream, pickle, olive, and anchovies!

green

red ①

2 green

3 green

4 red

green 5

6

7

8 purple

YUCKY

green

Level II

SILLY SCRIBBLE TEACHER-DIRECTED PAGE

LETTER RECOGNITION: Y y
SILLY SCRIBBLE: yak
PAPER DIRECTION: "lying down"
STAR COLOR: brown

TEACHER DIRECTIONS: Look for the number 1. This will tell you where to make the START line and what color to use.

- Keep in mind the basic strokes described in Section 1.
- Always use the whole paper when doing Silly Scribbles.
- Always write the name of the Silly Scribble or encourage the children to try and write it themselves.
- Emphasize to the children that this is only one way of making a yak. Discuss other ways.

QUESTIONS YOU COULD ASK:
- What kind of animal is this?
- Why do you think this animal needs so much fur?
- Which line did we make first? Last?
- What sound do you hear in the middle of the word "yak?"

ADDITIONAL ACTIVITIES:
- Think of words that rhyme with yak.
- After looking at pictures of where yaks live, discuss why yaks need heavy coats.
- Discuss the other meaning of "yak."

CREATIVE THINKING STARTERS:
- Write a collaborative story about the yak that was always "yakking."

SUGGESTED READING:
- *The Lucky Yak* by Annetta Lawson. Illustrated by Allen Say. Oakland, CA: Parnassus Press, 1980.

NOTES:

© 1989 by Shirley A. Steinmetz

all brown

fill in the area
with brown

brown

brown

Level III

YaK

SILLY SCRIBBLE TEACHER-DIRECTED PAGE

LETTER RECOGNITION: Z z
SILLY SCRIBBLE: zipper
PAPER DIRECTION: "standing up"
STAR COLOR: red

TEACHER DIRECTIONS: Look for the number 1. This will tell you where to make the START line and what color to use.

- Keep in mind the basic strokes described in Section 1.
- Always use the whole paper when doing Silly Scribbles.
- Always write the name of the Silly Scribble or encourage the children to try and write it themselves.
- Emphasize to the children that this is only one way of making a zipper. Discuss other ways.

QUESTIONS YOU COULD ASK:
- What was your first clue to what this Silly Scribble was?
- Do zippers only go up and down?
- What sound does "zipper" begin with? End with?

ADDITIONAL ACTIVITIES:
- Make a list of all the things that have zippers.
- What sound does a zipper make when it moves?
- Discuss different kinds of fasteners. Which is easiest to use?
- Let the children practice zipping their own coats and each other's coats.
- Bring in or ask parents to send in some zippers. Let the children examine and see how the zipper works. If you get enough variety, have the children sort them according to size, color, or type.

CREATIVE THINKING STARTERS:
- Make up a story to explain why or how the zipper was first invented.

SUGGESTED READING:
- *What to Do When Your Mom or Dad Says: "Get Dressed!"* by Joy W. Berry. Sebastosol, CA: Living Skills, 1982.
- *Oh Lewis*, story and pictures by Eve Rice. New York: Macmillan, 1974.
- *The Philharmonic Gets Dressed* by Karla Kuskin. Illustrated by Marc Simont. New York: Harper & Row, 1982.

NOTES:

 red

red ① 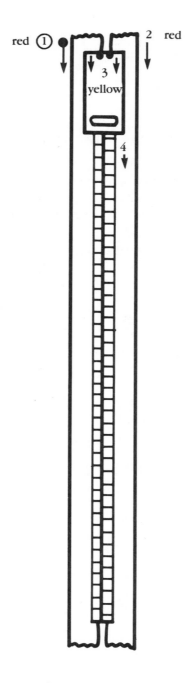 2 red

3
yellow

4

 zipper

Level I

SILLY SCRIBBLE TEACHER-DIRECTED PAGE

Level II

LETTER RECOGNITION: Z z
SILLY SCRIBBLE: zoo
PAPER DIRECTION: "lying down"
STAR COLOR: blue

TEACHER DIRECTIONS: Look for the number 1. This will tell you where to make the START line and what color to use.

- Keep in mind the basic strokes described in Section 1.
- Always use the whole paper when doing Silly Scribbles.
- Always write the name of the Silly Scribble or encourage the children to try and write it themselves.
- Emphasize to the children that this is only one way of making a zoo. Discuss other ways.

QUESTIONS YOU COULD ASK:

- What was your first clue that this Silly Scribble would be the word "zoo"?
- Have the children fill in the letters with animals they have seen or would see in a zoo.

ADDITIONAL ACTIVITIES:

- Take a trip to a nearby zoo.
- Play "I'm thinking of. . ." Let the children act out or give clues to tell what animal they are thinking of.
- Have "Zoo Day" and encourage the children to come dressed as zoo animals.
- Have the children make pictures of different zoo families.

CREATIVE THINKING STARTERS:

- Think of a new kind of zoo animal. Make a picture of it. How about a striped lion? A polka-dotted elephant?

SUGGESTED READING:

- *If I Ran a Zoo* by Dr. Seuss. New York: Random House, 1950.
- *A Trip Through the Zoo* by Phyllis Jean Perry. Illustrated by Barbara Furan. Minneapolis: T. S. Denison and Co., 1968.

NOTES:

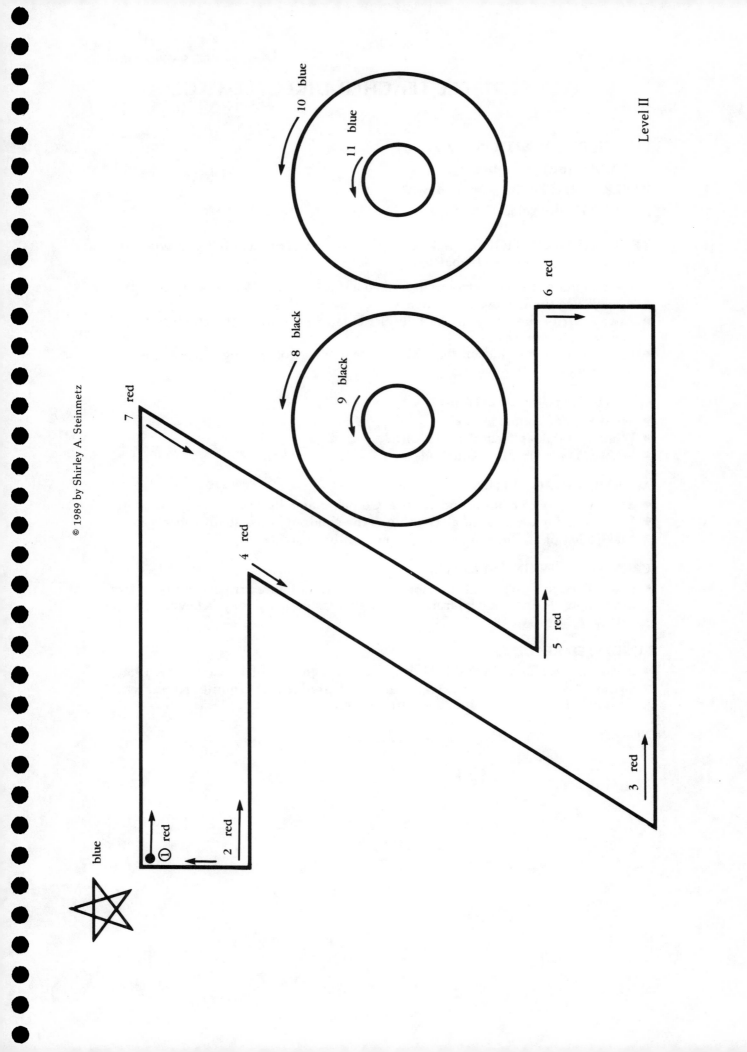

© 1989 by Shirley A. Steinmetz

Level II

SILLY SCRIBBLE TEACHER-DIRECTED PAGE

LETTER RECOGNITION: Z z
SILLY SCRIBBLE: zebra
PAPER DIRECTION: "lying down"
STAR COLOR: black

TEACHER DIRECTIONS: Look for the number 1. This will tell you where to make the START line and what color to use.

- Keep in mind the basic strokes described in Section 1.
- Always use the whole paper when doing Silly Scribbles.
- Always write the name of the Silly Scribble or encourage the children to try and write it themselves.
- Emphasize to the children that this is only one way of making a zebra. Discuss other ways.

QUESTIONS YOU COULD ASK:

- What kind of animal is this?
- What sound does "zebra" begin with?
- What was the first line you made?

ADDITIONAL ACTIVITIES:

- Show pictures of a horse and a zebra. Compare and discuss.
- Discuss and make a list of all the things the children know about zebras.
- Make a list of all the animals you know that have stripes.

CREATIVE THINKING STARTERS:

- Is a zebra white with black stripes, or black with white stripes? Have a class discussion, letting the children share their reasons why they believe the way they do.

SUGGESTED READING:

- *Zella, Zack, and Zodiac* by Bill Peet. Boston: Houghton Mifflin Company, 1986.
- *Greedy Zebra* by Mwenye Hadithi. Illustrated by Adrienne Kennaway. Boston: Little, Brown and Company, 1984.

NOTES:

© 1989 by Shirley A. Steinmetz

19 stripes

all black

black

green grass

Level III

zebra

Section 3
FRIENDS

(a reproducible individual book to take home and tell)

Use this story to introduce Stan and Carla to your class. The children will enjoy following the lines of dots and dashes to make the pictures on the cover and in their very own book. (Extra copies should be made to keep in the classroom for the children to look at and read often.)

Explain that this is their very own copy of *Friends* and they should keep it in a special place to read again. After reading the story to the children, let them have their very own stapled copy. Have the children get a green crayon and a blue crayon and trace over the lines on the cover. Take as much time as needed to do the pages before sending it home with the children. Encourage them to read or tell the story to their families.

Section 3 consists of:
- the cover for *Friends*
- letter to parents
- the story
- suggested activities for parents and children

Stan and Carla
in
Friends

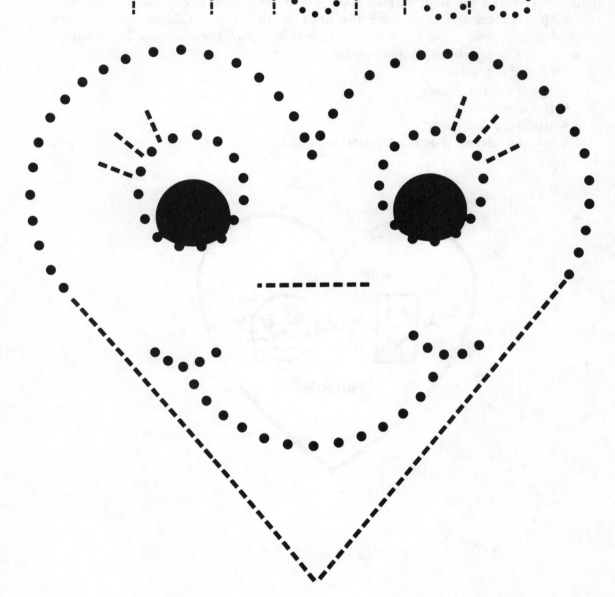

You are special too!

Let's be friends!

Dear Parents,

    You and your child will be reading a story about a straight line named "Stan" and a curved line named "Carla."

    Reading this story with your child should open up many areas for discussion. *Friends* introduces colors, shapes, numbers, letters, pictures, feelings, and especially the concept that each of us has a special "something" that makes each person different.

    During the course of this school year, Stan and Carla will be your child's special friends. Your child will use Stan and Carla in many different ways to reinforce the many basic readiness skills for use in written language. One of the many fun activities is "Silly Scribbles." Here your child will use Stan straight lines and Carla curved lines to make pictures. This is a success-oriented program where your child will simply play follow-the-leader with crayons. While doing this, many of the following skills will be reinforced: left-to-right movement, colors, shapes, numbers, eye-hand coordination, fine-motor reinforcement, spatial placement, and predicting outcome.

    So it is our hope that you will encourage your child to discuss Stan and Carla with you by reading this story again and again throughout this school year.

_____
Teacher

Let's play follow the leader!

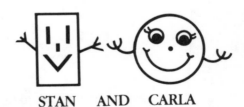

STAN   AND   CARLA

Once there was a straight line named Stan.

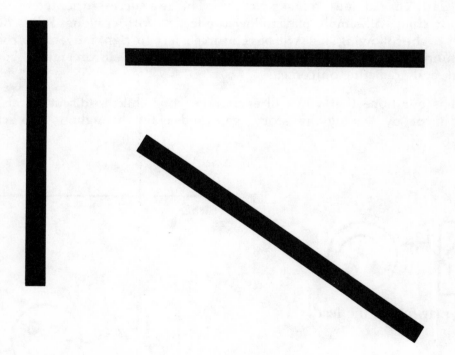

Stan could go down, left-to-right, or slant.

Stan straight line could make many things!

T V Z

Stan could make LETTERS. . .

H

7 4 |

. . .and NUMBERS!

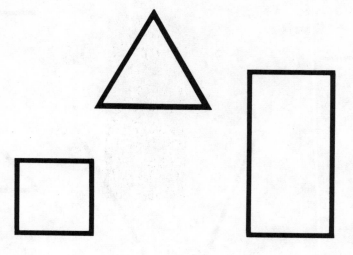

Stan could make SHAPES!

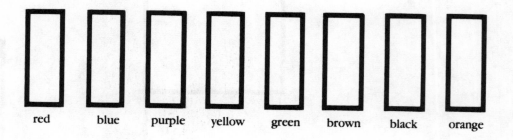

red   blue   purple   yellow   green   brown   black   orange

Stan straight line came in many different COLORS, too!

(Fill in the Stan straight lines with the correct color.)

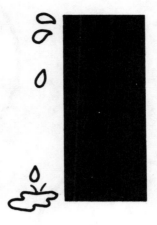

But Stan straight line was not very happy!

Just then, along came his good friend, Carla curve.

Now, Carla curve could also make LETTERS. . .

. . .and NUMBERS!

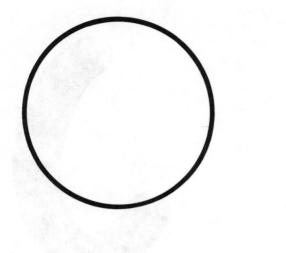

Carla curve could make the SHAPES circle and oval.

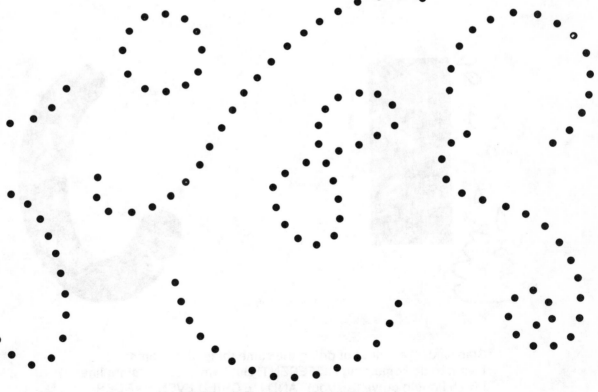

And Carla also came in COLORS!

(Trace over the dotted Carla lines using one of each color: red, blue, purple, green, brown, black, orange, and yellow).

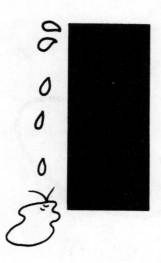 

When Carla saw that her good friend Stan was not very happy, she asked him to tell her why he was SO sad.

Stan said, "I am tired of doing the same thing all the time!
I want to do something DIFFERENT! But I am only a straight line!
I wish I could curve like you!" AND HE CRIED EVEN HARDER!

Carla thought for a minute. Then she said, "Stan, you can do some things, and I can do others. Why don't we play TOGETHER and see what we can do!"

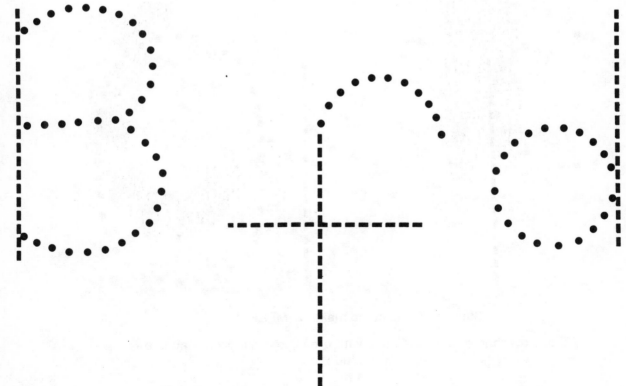

So Stan and Carla began to play. Together they could make LETTERS!

(Trace over the dotted Carla line with green, and the dash Stan line with blue.)

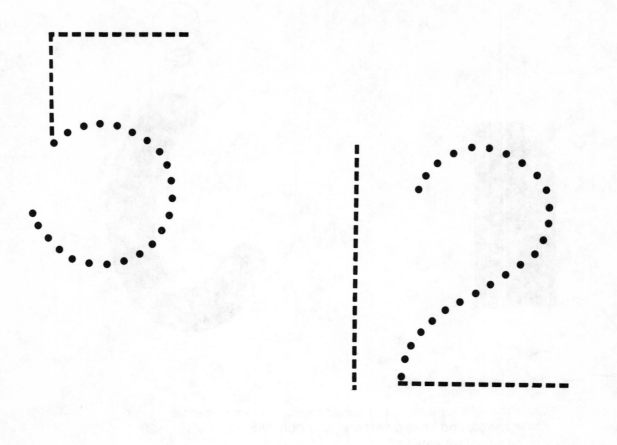

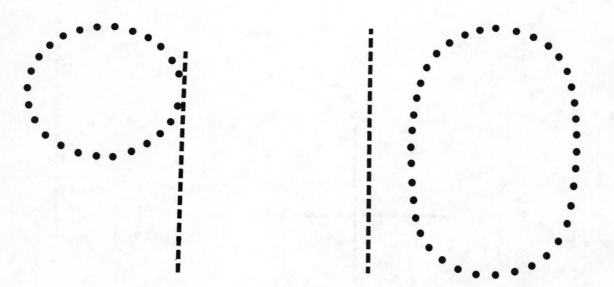

Stan and Carla could make NUMBERS!

(Trace over the dotted Carla line with green, and the <u>dash</u> Stan line
with blue.)

Stan and Carla could make PEOPLE!

(Trace over the dotted Carla line with green, and the <u>dash</u> Stan line with blue.)

Now Stan is HAPPY, because he and Carla can make beautiful PICTURES!

(Trace over the dotted Carla line with green, and the <u>dash</u> Stan line with blue.)

I Love you!

Stan and Carla lived happily ever after!

THE END

(Trace over the dotted Carla line with green, and the dash Stan line
with blue.)

SUGGESTED ACTIVITIES
FOR PARENTS AND CHILDREN

1. Save this story to read again and again.

2. Look everywhere! Your clothes, toys, room, shoes, crayons, paper, face, in books, rocks, windows, doors, trees, clouds—anywhere—and find "Stan" and "Carla" lines. Touch and feel them if you can.

3. Look at the different foods you eat and see which have "Stan" and "Carla" lines. Carrots can be cut into "Stan" or "Carla" shapes.

4. When writing your child's name, look at the letters and point out the "Stan" and "Carla" lines.

5. Encourage your child to make a picture using "Stan" and "Carla" lines. Can they tell you which is which?

6. Play "Where Is Stan?" (or Carla?) Make a small posterboard Stan (or Carla) and while your child covers his or her eyes, hide Stan (or Carla) somewhere in the room. Let some part stick out so your child can see where it is by looking. See if your child can tell where it is hidden using words that tell direction or placement, such as "Stan is *under* the red apple," or "Stan is *behind* the teddy bear." Then let your child hide Stan (or Carla) from you. Take turns, reinforcing verbal skills. Your child will enjoy this game while it encourages him or her to use whole sentences and basic comprehension skills.

7. When playing with blocks, puzzles, shapes, beads, and the like, sort them into three piles: those made by Stan alone, those made by Carla alone, or those made by Stan and Carla together. Let your child "feel" the difference, try it with eyes closed. This helps with sorting and classifying skills.

HAVE FUN!

Section 4

STAN AND CARLA CLOSURE ALPHABET

These reproducible worksheets can be copied for each child or run off and laminated for children to use again and again. Unlike the story *Friends* that is recommended for use at the beginning of the year, these worksheets can be done in any order or at any time you feel fits best with your program.

Each worksheet will have:

- one letter per page in both upper case and lower case Aa

- a picture of who makes the letter

    -- Stan makes these letters by himself (A E F H I K L M N T V W X Y Z k l t v w x y z)

    -- Carla makes these letters by herself (C O S c o s)

    -- Stan and Carla make these letters together (B D G J P Q R U a b d e f g h i j m n p q r u)

    -- Stan makes the first line in these letters (B D J P R U b h j i m n p r u)

    -- Carla makes the first line in these letters (G Q a d e f g q)

- a star in the left-hand corner for the child's name

- a sun for the child to write the date

- an example of the letters to help the child remember what the letter should look like and a beginning sound picture

- a practice line on which to make the letters

★ NAME _____

☀ DATE _____

Follow the Stan and Carla
lines to make the letters.

Acorn

Aa

Apple

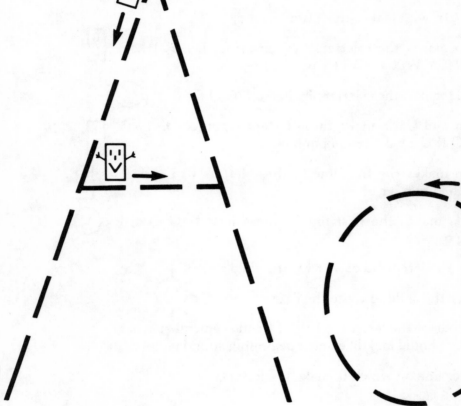

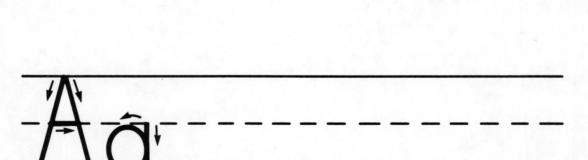

Visual closure A a

Follow the Stan and Carla
lines to make the letters.

Bear

B b

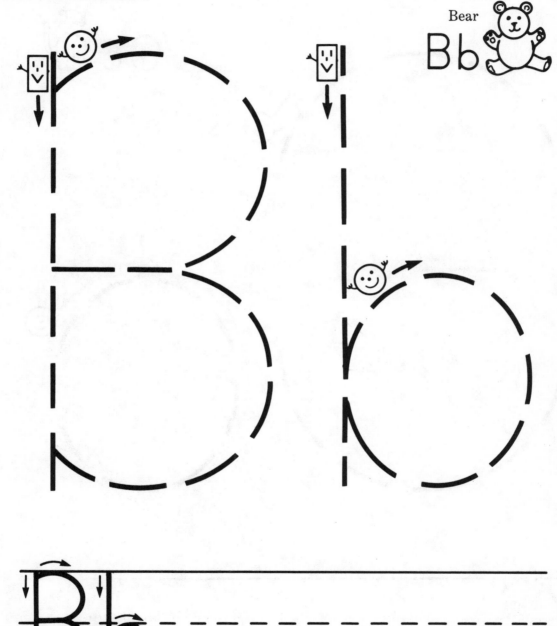

Visual closure B b

Follow the Stan and Carla
lines to make the letters.

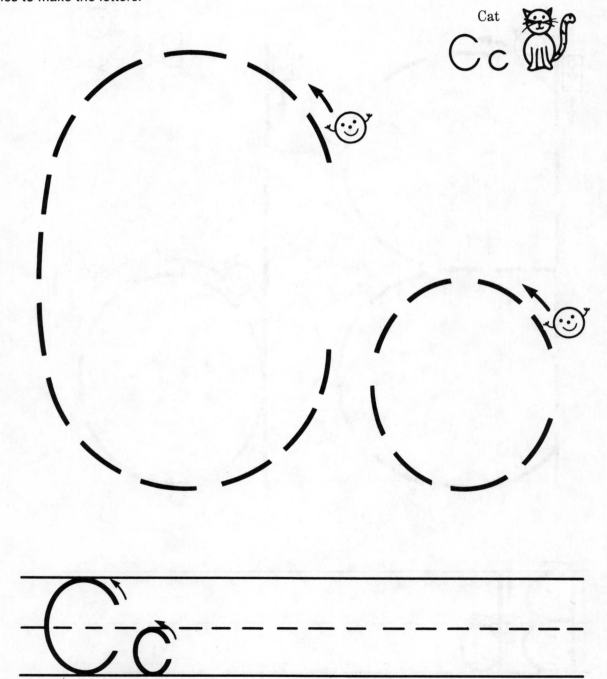

Cat

C c

C c

Visual closure C c

NAME _____

DATE _____

Follow the Stan and Carla lines to make the letters.

Dog

Dd

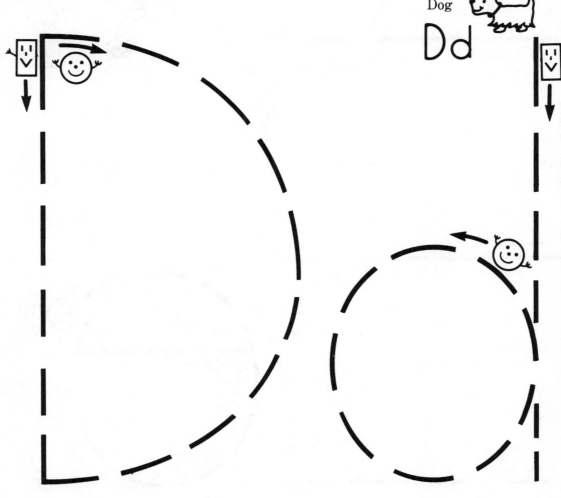

Visual closure D d

Follow the Stan and Carla
lines to make the letters.

Egg   Ear

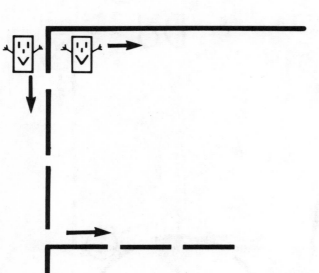

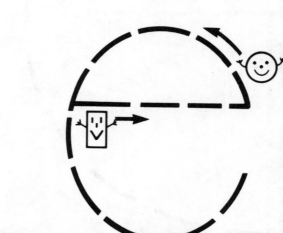

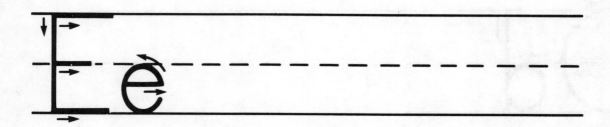

© 1989 by Shirley A. Steinmetz

Visual closure E e

Follow the Stan and Carla
lines to make the letters.

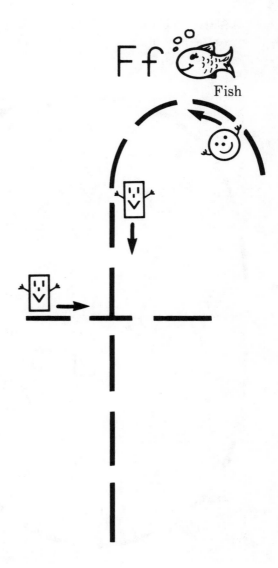

Fish

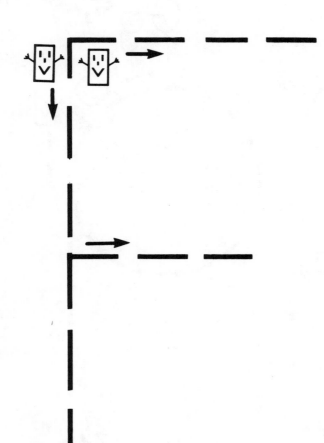

Visual closure F f

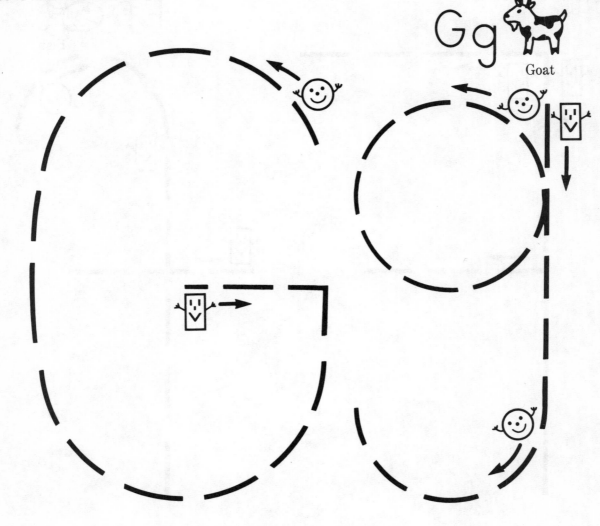
NAME _____

DATE _____

Follow the Stan and Carla
lines to make the letters.

Gg

Goat

© 1989 by Shirley A. Steinmetz

Visual closure G g

Follow the Stan and Carla
lines to make the letters.

House

Hh

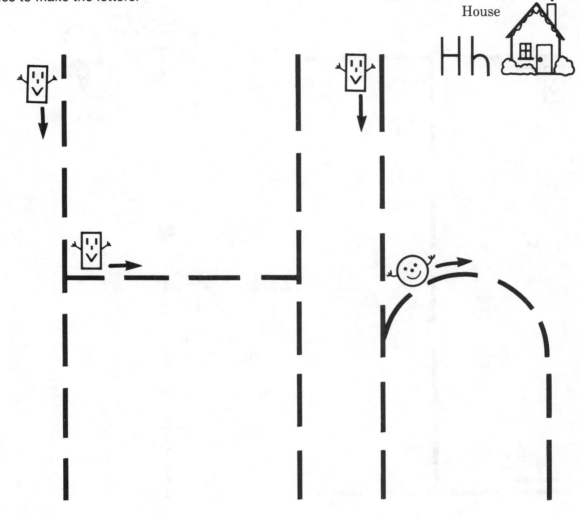

Visual closure H h

Follow the Stan lines to
make the letters. Use Carla for the dot.

Igloo

Ice cream

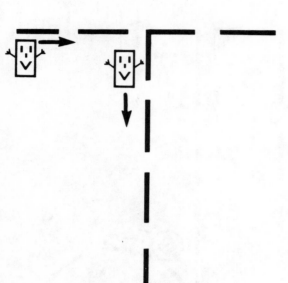

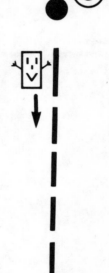

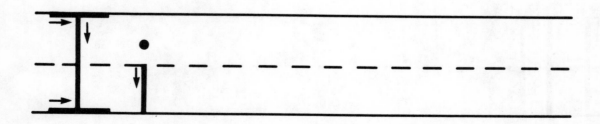

Visual closure I i

NAME

DATE

Follow the Stan and Carla
lines to make the letters.

Jacket

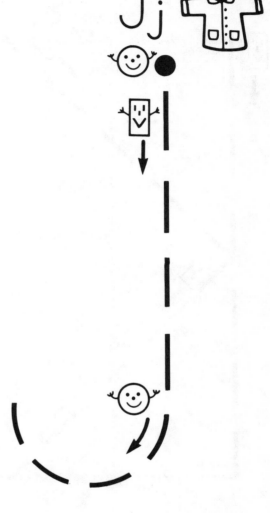

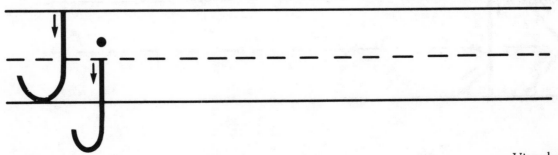

Visual closure J j

Follow the Stan straight
and slide lines to make the letters.

Kite

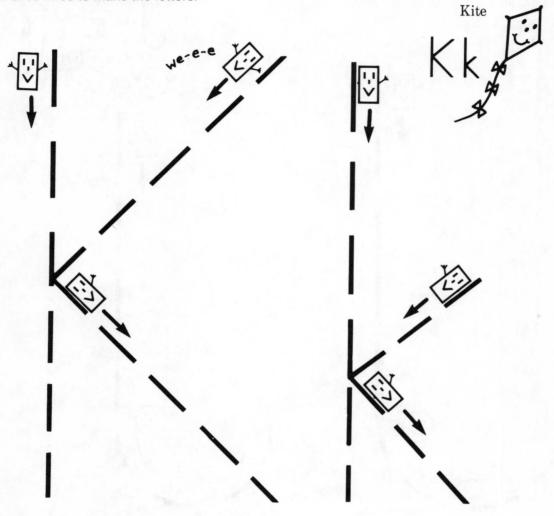

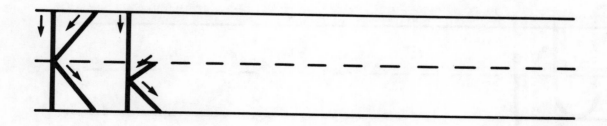

Visual closure K k

Follow the Stan lines
to make the letters.

L l

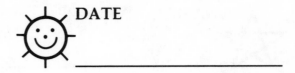

Lion

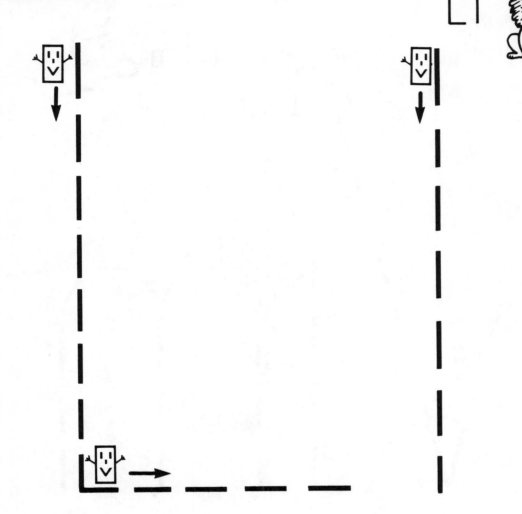

Visual closure L l

Follow the Stan and Carla
lines to make the letters.

Mouse

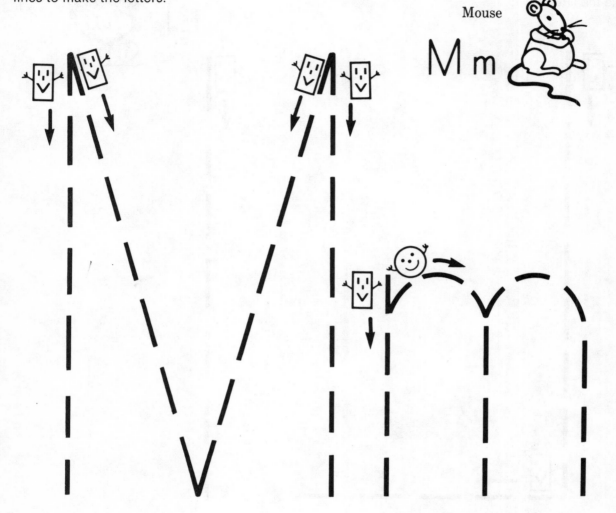

Visual closure M m

Follow the Stan and Carla
lines to make the letters.

Nest

Nn

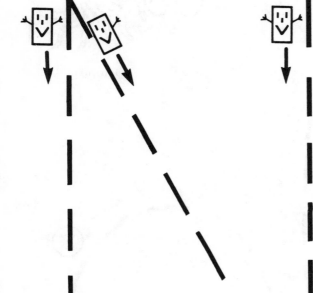

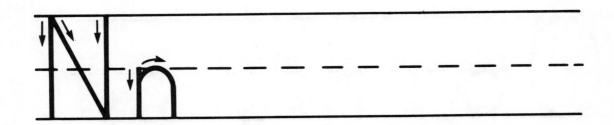

Visual closure N n

Follow the Carla curve
lines to make the letters.

Oar

Octopus

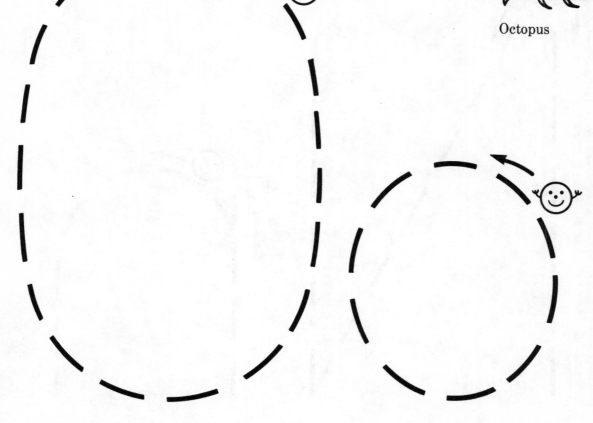

Visual closure O o

Follow the Stan and Carla
lines to make the letters.

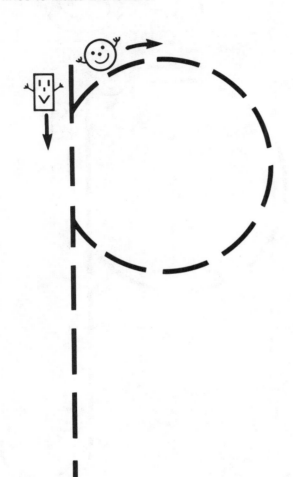

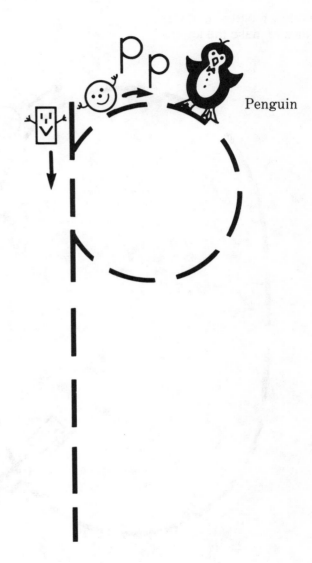

Penguin

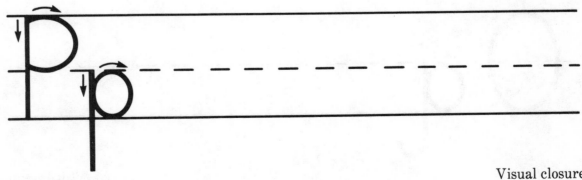

Visual closure P p

Follow the Stan and Carla
lines to make the letters.

Quail

Q q

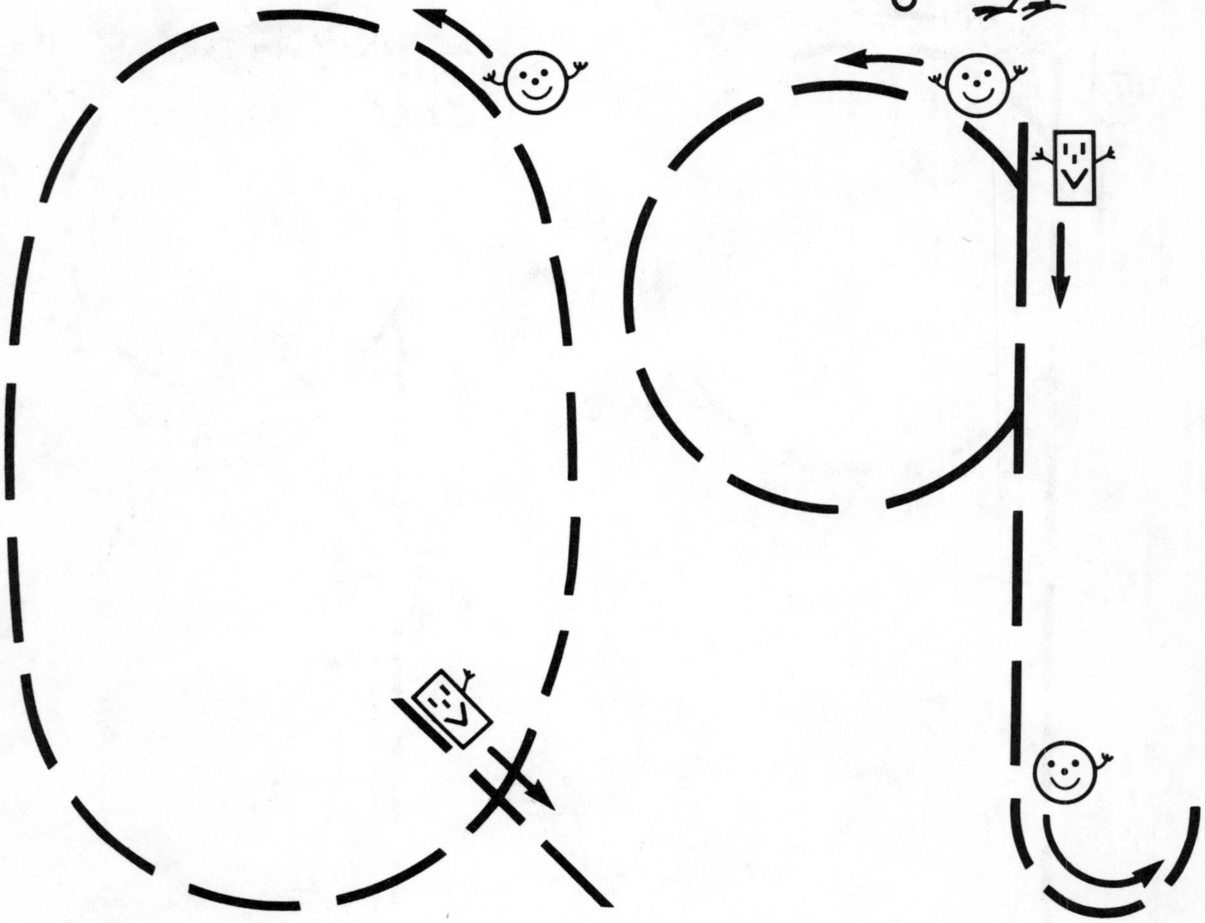

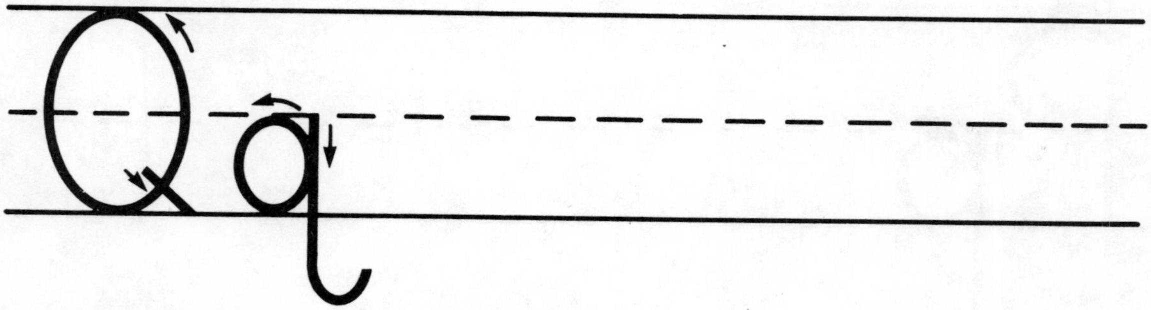

Visual closure Q q

Follow the Stan and Carla
lines to make the letters.

Rabbit

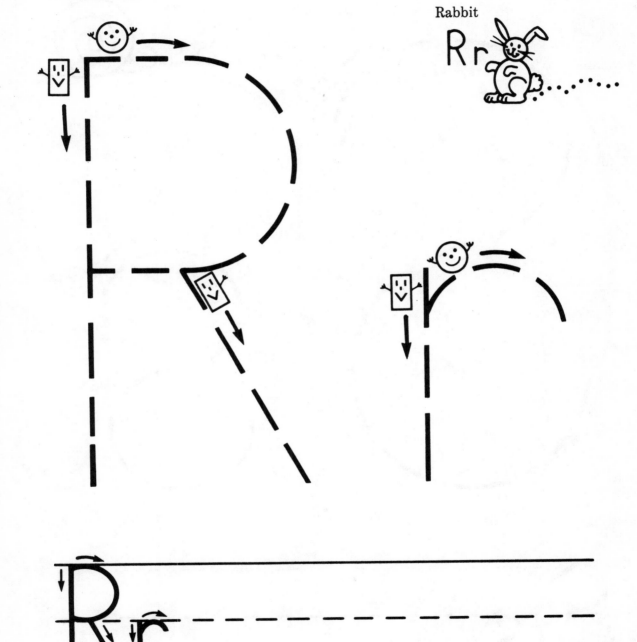

Visual closure R r

Follow the Carla curve
line to make the letters.

Snail

S s

S s

© 1989 by Shirley A. Steinmetz

Visual closure S s

 NAME _____

DATE _____

Follow the Stan straight
lines to make the letters.

Turtle

T t

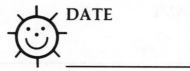

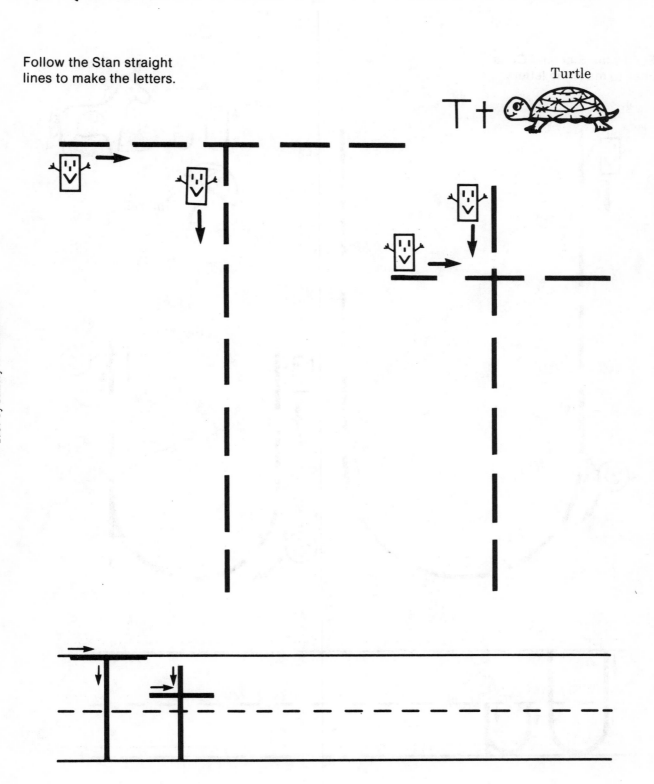

Visual closure T t

Follow the Stan and Carla
lines to make the letters.

Unicorn

Umbrella

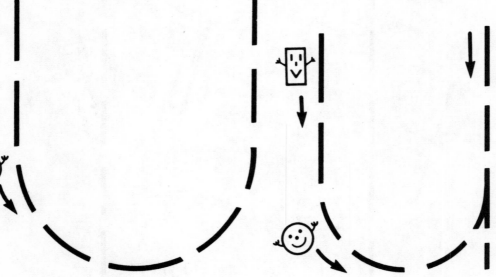

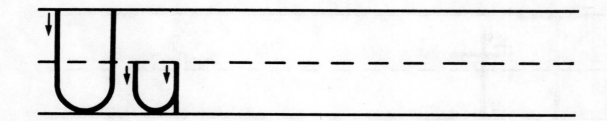

Visual closure U u

Follow the Stan slide
lines to make the letters.

Valentine

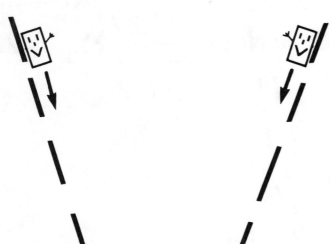

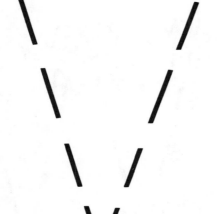

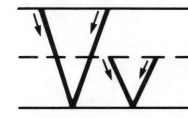

Visual closure V v

Follow the Stan slide
lines to make the letters.

Walrus

W w

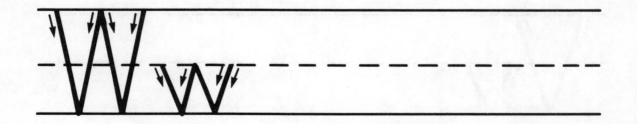

© 1989 by Shirley A. Steinmetz

Visual closure W w

 **NAME** _____

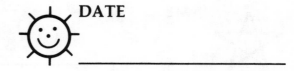 **DATE** _____

Follow the Stan slide
lines to make the letters.

X-Ray

X x

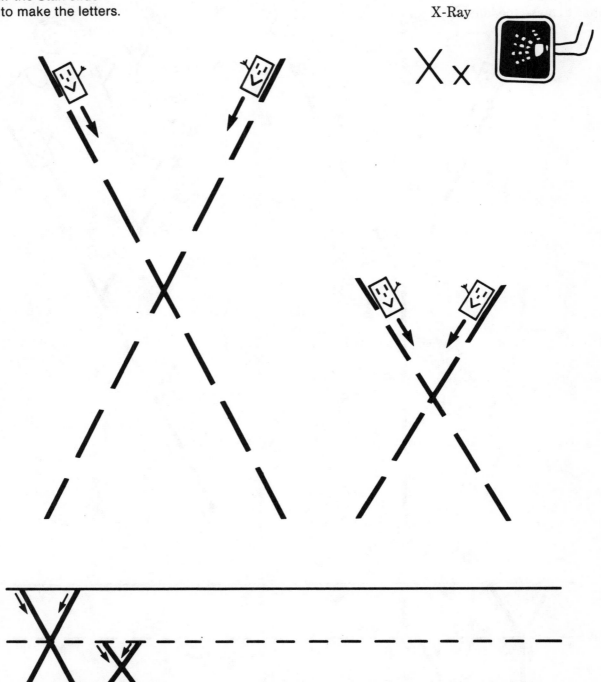

Visual closure X x

Follow the Stan
lines to make the letters.

Yo-yo

Y y

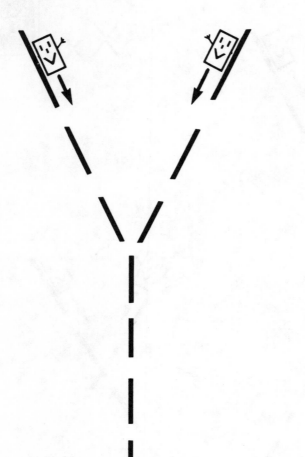

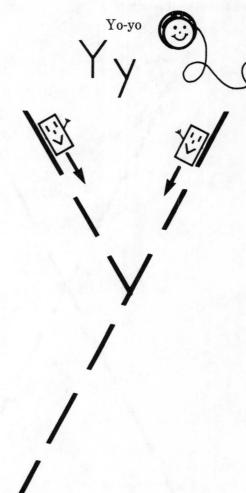

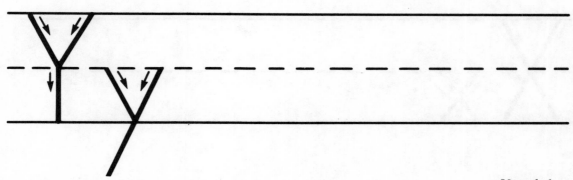

Visual closure Y y

Follow the Stan lines
to make the letters.

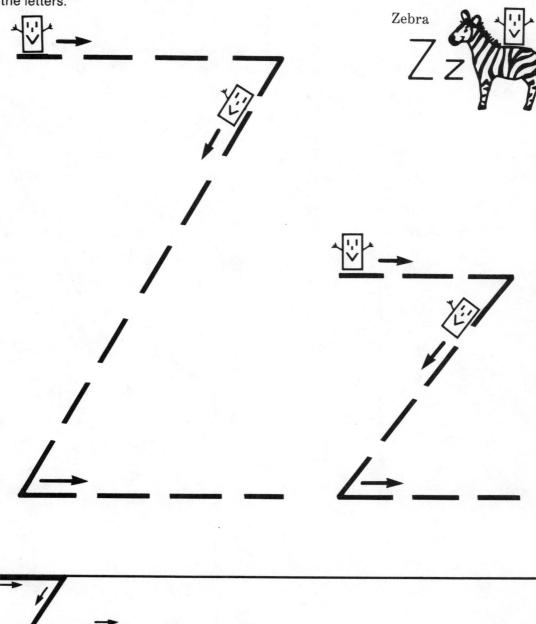

Zebra

Z z

Visual closure Z z